I hope you find
in this genuine facsimile autograph
an actual replica of my
sincerest personal regards.
Ashleigh
Brilliant

Books by Ashleigh Brilliant

(all published by Woodbridge Press)

Books of Brilliant Thoughts:®

I. I MAY NOT BE TOTALLY PERFECT, BUT PARTS OF ME ARE EXCELLENT© (1979).

II. I HAVE ABANDONED MY SEARCH FOR TRUTH, AND AM NOW LOOKING FOR A GOOD FANTASY© (1980).

III. APPRECIATE ME NOW, AND AVOID THE RUSH© (1981).

IV. I FEEL MUCH BETTER, NOW THAT I'VE GIVEN UP HOPE© (1984).

V. ALL I WANT IS A WARM BED AND A KIND WORD, AND UNLIMITED POWER© (1985).

VI. I TRY TO TAKE ONE DAY AT A TIME, BUT SOMETIMES SEVERAL DAYS ATTACK ME AT ONCE© (1987).

VII. WE'VE BEEN THROUGH SO MUCH TOGETHER — AND MOST OF IT WAS YOUR FAULT© (1990).

Other Books:

The Great Car Craze: How Southern California Collided with the Automobile in the 1920's (1989).

We've Been Through So MuchTogether,
and *MOST OF IT WAS YOUR FAULT.*©

More and More
BRILLIANT THOUGHTS®
by

Ashleigh Brilliant

Woodbridge Press
Santa Barbara, California 93160

1992

Published by
Woodbridge Press Publishing Company
Post Office Box 6189
Santa Barbara, California 93160

Copyright © 1990, by Ashleigh Brilliant

All rights reserved.

Distributed simultaneously in the United States and Canada.

Printed in the United States of America.

Library of Congress Cataloging-in-Publication Data

Brilliant, Ashleigh, 1933-
  We've been through so much together, and most of it was your fault: more Brilliant Thoughts/ by Ashleigh Brilliant
  p. cm.
ISBN 0-88007-182-6: $12.95—ISBN 0-88007-183-4 (pbk.): $.795

1. Epigrams, American. 2. American wit and humor, pictorial.

I. Title. II. Title: We've been through so much together, and most of it was your fault.
PN6281.B685 1900
818'k.5402—dc20   90-12357
                                                    CIP

POT SHOTS® *and BRILLIANT THOUGHTS*®
are Registered Trade Marks.

Dedication

To my wife Dorothy,
who is so much a part of everything I do.

YOUR SMILE IS ONE OF THE GREAT SIGHTS OF THE WORLD*

*POT-SHOT #980

Acknowledgements

Special thanks to:

Sue McMillan, a great helper, for being involved in all this for so long.

My cousin, Barry Cantor, U.S.A.F., for making Berlin even more extraordinary.

Walter McQuesten, for the beautiful experience of Barrow, Alaska.

Richard Holden, D.M.V., for distinguished curing of cats and computers.

Steven Gilbar, Attorney-at-Law, for friendship beyond the call of Copyright protection.

Paul Lenze, for many years, and many kinds, of help and care.

My faithful friend Allen Carrico, for devoted distribution.

My mother Amelia Brilliant, for my existence, and so much more.

Howard, Dorothy, and Caroline Weeks, of Woodbridge Press, for always wanting another Brilliant book.

Dorothy Brilliant, for heroic wifing.

Sol Morrison, for he's a jolly good fellow.

And also to:

Jon Thornburgh, Ruth Dayes, Wayne Gertmenian, Bonnie Edelstein, Marianne Partridge, Fred Salter, Barry Gantt, "Choyous" Chin Kean Choy, Richard Long, Ralph Sipper, Brandy Brandon, Jay Bail, Ness Carroll, Anne D'Arcy, Madeleine Walker, Gene Gumplo, Susan Hosch, Don McDonald, Robert Pepper, Don Voegele, Barney Brantingham, Norman Cohan, Dolly Winton, Joan Crowder, Father David Carriere, Pauline Meyer, Mary Kana, Woodrow and Marie Ohlsen, Audrey Ovington, Hilda and Adrian Wenner, Dr. Tod Forman, Martha U. Wellington, James Geiwitz, Douglas R. Hofstadter, Marjorie Low, Bonnie May Malody, and Donald B. Ardell

— each of whom (for better or worse) has played an important and much-appreciated part in helping and encouraging me to keep having Brilliant Thoughts®

Contents

Books by Ashleigh Brilliant *2*
Dedication *5*
Acknowledgements *6*
Introduction: *9*

    Hello Forever© *9*
    Whining Over Signing *10*
    Profit Without Honor *11*
    Gloating Over Quoting *12*
    Alphabet Gravy *14*
    Of Theme I Sing *14*
    Getting Somewhere *15*
    Running to Seed *17*
    Fault Line *17*

   I. Self Starter *19*
  II. Thee, We, and Me *31*
 III. Human Nature Trail *43*
 IV. Familiar Terms *55*
  V. Inter Play *67*
 VI. World of Difference *79*
 VII. Life and the Other Thing *91*
VIII. Mind Over Mutter *103*
 IX. Time Pieces *115*
  X. Lost and Profound *127*
 XI. Another Think Coming *139*
 XII. Light at the End *151*

Appendix 1: Copy Catch *162*
Appendix 2: Fan Mail and Pan Mail *164*

Loose End *167*

The Secretary of State
of the United States of America
hereby requests all whom it may concern to permit the citizen/
national of the United States named herein to pass
without delay or hindrance and in case of need to
give all lawful aid and protection.

Le Secrétaire d'Etat
des Etats-Unis d'Amérique
prie par les présentes toutes autorités compétentes de laisser passer
le citoyen ou ressortissant des Etats-Unis titulaire du présent passeport,
sans délai ni difficulté et, en cas de besoin, de lui accorder
toute aide et protection légitimes.

SIGNATURE OF BEARER/SIGNATURE DU TITULAIRE

UNITED STATES OF AMERICA

PASSPORT PASSEPORT	Type/Caté-gorie **P** Code of issuing / code du pays State USA émetteur PASSPORT NO./NO. DU PASSEPORT **030932993**

Surname / Nom
BRILLIANT
Given names / Prénoms
ASHLEIGH ELLWOOD
Nationality / Nationalité
UNITED STATES OF AMERICA
Date of birth / Date de naissance
09 DEC/DEC 33
Sex / Sexe   Place of birth / Lieu de naissance
M   **UNITED KINGDOM**
Date of issue / Date de délivrance   Date of expiration / Date d'expiration
13 JUN/JUN 84   **12 JUN/JUN 94**
Authority / Autorité   Amendments/Modifications
PASSPORT AGENCY   SEE PAGE
LOS ANGELES   **24**

```
P<USABRILLIANT<ASHLEIGH<ELLWOOD<<<<<<<<<<<<<
0309329936USA3312094M9406122<<<<<<<<<<<<<<<6
```

We've Been Through So Much Together,
and Most of it Was Your Fault.©

Introduction

Yes, of course it's your fault, if you must keep getting involved with these oddball books! Nevertheless, let me welcome you aboard yet another erratic excursion from wherever your mind is currently located to wherever it can converge with mine. If you have already survived an encounter with any or all of the other books in this series, you honor (and in some ways you astonish) me by returning to the arena. But what is it that you really want this time? More of the same, I suppose — only different, and if possible even better. Fortunately for all concerned, that happens to be exactly what I have available.

Hello Forever[1]

But if by chance we have not met before, I feel I owe you at least a cursory briefing, to help you get your bearings on this unfamiliar terrain. First (since it is usually what I am asked first) know that Ashleigh Brilliant is the real name of a real person, and that he is I. (For verification, see Passport, opposite.) Nobody else (I think) can make that claim — nor can anybody else claim, as I do with some passion, to be the sole author and legal owner of all the epigrams called POT-SHOTS® and also known as BRILLIANT THOUGHTS,® of which this book is my seventh published collection.

I have to dwell on this proprietorship because, before I began to write and copyright them in 1967, short writings such as these (and mine never exceed 17 words) were more often scrawled on walls than published in books. Usually anonymous, they were accorded very little respect by cultivated critics. My aim has been to change all that, to prove that literary quality is not a matter of mere length, and to carve out what is apparently still a unique career as a professional creator of meritoriously minimal messages?[2]

---

[1]#1395. Individual copyrighted epigrams will be cited herein by Pot-Shot No. References to other books of "Brilliant Thoughts"® are by Book No. (see list, page 2).

[2]For copyright details, see "Appendix 1, COPY CATCH," p. 162.

To emphasize the self-contained nature of each of these epigrams, I began by publishing them, not in books, but individually on postcards, of which so many millions are by now in circulation that it is still the card form in which you are most likely first to come across my works, perhaps by receiving one in the mail from a friend. If you read the small print cunningly inserted on the back of the card, you might have been induced to send for a catalogue, which would make you aware of a vast array of these illustrated expressions, covering every imaginable feeling and situation, all easily available on postcards and in various other forms. (For exciting catalogue details herein, see LOOSE END, page 167.)

As to who is responsible for the illustrations, there also I plead guilty, and I hope they add to the fun without getting in the way of the meaning of my words. But these are epigrams, not cartoons. The words are (or should be) quite capable of standing by themselves, and, as far as ultimate recognition of my contribution to world culture is concerned, my sights are still fixed, not on the Louvre, but on the Nobel Prize for Literature.

Just how to assess my progress in that direction has always been problematic. If proliferation of licensed products and other permitted usages of my work were any indication, I should by now, propelled by piles of T-shirts, mugs, plaques, and numerous other such items — to say nothing of syndication in a scad of newspapers — be well on my way to Stockholm. If lavish praise in the form of fan mail (all of it cherished and carefully preserved) were any criterion, I would long since have been seated among the Immortals. (I feel you should see some evidence of this, but have modestly relegated it to an Appendix. See "Appendix 2: FAN MAIL AND PAN MAIL," page 164.)

Whining Over Signing

But proliferation and praise, no matter how spectacular, are hardly the most reliable gauges of success. My antennae are therefore always tuned to other indicators. One of these, concerning which I have lately been getting some very mixed signals, is the market value of my autograph.

In May 1989, an internationally-reputed firm of rare-book dealers[3] obtained an autographed copy of the 1979 hardbound first edition of my first book, of which only 1,000 copies had been printed, and offered it in their catalogue at a price of $150. This in itself was impressive, being as much as, and in some

[3]Joseph the Provider, of Santa Barbara — telephone (805) 962-6862.

cases more than, was being charged in the same list for signed first editions of works by H.L. Mencken, Samuel Beckett, Saul Bellow, Eudora Welty, John Updike, John Irving, and Norman Mailer. But unfortunately (and despite strong hints which I sent out to some of my more fervent fans) as of this writing, the item remains unsold.

That same price of $150, however, actually was paid for a signed doodle I had been invited to provide for a "Celebrity Doodle Auction" in aid of Santa Barbara's Lobero Theater, held on February 10, 1990. This was quite comforting until the purchaser (whom I did not know), confessed, when I called to thank him, that his primary motivation had not been any special admiration for me, but a desire to help the Theater at a figure he could afford (since nearly all the other celebrities' works had sold for much higher amounts).

Then there was the case of another fund-raising auction, this time for the benefit of our local City College, to which I donated a signed custom-made POT-SHOT® which was supposed to be drawn, sometime after the auction, specially for the purchaser. I did not attend the event, which was held in November 1988, but was later told that the POT-SHOT® had actually sold for $250! This too would have been cause for exultation, but for the fact that whoever bought it has, to this day, never bothered to claim it.

And I am even more puzzled by what happened when I presented a personally-inscribed copy of one of my books to my barber, who left it out on a table in his shop for the entertainment of other customers. Some time later he discovered that, although the book was still there, somebody had torn out the page containing the autograph and presumably purloined it. Of course, I can't be sure exactly what motivated this audacious act. But it does afford me the hope that, even if I'm not yet really worth buying, or, if bought, even worth claiming, I may at least, to somebody somewhere, be worth stealing.

Profit Without Honor

Another possible measure of success derives from one of my favorite fantasies — that one day I will be invited back, to be received with honor and acclaim, by all the schools and colleges where I once studied or taught, and where my greatness was so little recognized or appreciated at the time.[4] The single occasion on which that dream has so far come closest to

[4]There have so far been at least 17 of them:
Dollis Hill Nursery School, London (1938-39); Brock Avenue School, Toronto (1939-40); Williamson Road School, Toronto (1940); Grace Street School, Toronto

fulfilment occurred in September 1987, when I actually did appear by special invitation as a featured speaker on the campus of the University of California at Berkeley, in Dwinelle Hall, home of the very History department in which I had toiled for four years as an obscure graduate student and teaching assistant.

Unfortunately, however, the event had nothing to do with that department, or even with the University at all, which was merely providing the space. It was a conference sponsored by the San Francisco Cartoon Art Museum, and I was there, not (as I would have much preferred) to acknowledge a grateful, if belated, tribute from my Alma Mater, but merely to share my mundane expertise on "Designing and Marketing the Greeting Card." Still, as you can see, my particular fantasy-world is one in which you take what you can get.

Gloating Over Quoting

But there *are* other forms of recognition, and, since the appearance of my last book, I have in fact received at least one extraordinary and very public accolade. The chances are, however, that you never noticed it, so please pay close attention to the following:

As you may know, the Reader's Digest, a monthly which claims to be "the world's most-read magazine," regularly features a page entitled "Quotable Quotes." Considering the eminence of many of its quotees (the likes of William Shakespeare, Benjamin Franklin, Abraham Lincoln, and Mark Twain), of whom only about a dozen are selected each month, even one appearance therein might be considered the height of any utterer's ambition. I myself actually achieved that triumph for the first time in June 1980[5] and it happened again in July 1983. But beginning in March 1988, the pace quickened dramatically, and from then through April 1989, yours truly found himself in "Quotable Quotes" no fewer than FIVE times! I was so impressed by this flattering tribute that I took the trouble to make a statistical analysis of the feature, and you can imagine with what glee I discovered that, during that 14-

(1940-41); Whittier Elementary School, Washington D.C. (1941-44); Paul Junior High School, Washington D.C. (1944-46); Portchester Road Secondary School, Bournemouth, England (1946); Hendon County Grammar School, London (1947-52) University College, London (1952-55); Los Angeles State College (1956); Claremont Graduate School, California (1956-57); Hollywood High School, Los Angeles (1957-58); San Jose State College, California (1958-59); University of California, Berkeley (1960-64); San Joaquin Delta College, Stockton, California (1964); Central Oregon Community College, Bend, Oregon (1964-65); Chapman College (Seven Seas Division), Orange, California (1965-67).

[5]See Book III, p. 13.

AGUDATH ACHIM HEBREW SCHOOL
909 QUACKENBOS STREET, N. W.
WASHINGTON, D. C.
TAYLOR 5720

November 11, 1942

Class Report
For

Avrohom Brilliant

Good student in every sense of the word.

H. Waldman

THE REGENTS OF THE UNIVERSITY OF CALIFORNIA

ON THE NOMINATION OF THE
GRADUATE COUNCIL OF THE BERKELEY DIVISION
HAVE CONFERRED UPON

ASHLEIGH ELLWOOD BRILLIANT

WHO HAS PROVED HIS ABILITY BY ORIGINAL RESEARCH
IN HISTORY
THE DEGREE OF DOCTOR OF PHILOSOPHY
WITH ALL THE RIGHTS AND PRIVILEGES THERETO PERTAINING

GIVEN AT BERKELEY THIS TWENTY-NINTH DAY OF JANUARY
IN THE YEAR NINETEEN HUNDRED AND SIXTY-FOUR

Edmund G. Brown
GOVERNOR OF CALIFORNIA AND
PRESIDENT OF THE REGENTS

Clark Kerr
PRESIDENT OF THE UNIVERSITY

EK Strong
CHANCELLOR AT BERKELEY

Sanford S. Elberg
DEAN OF THE GRADUATE DIVISION
AT BERKELEY

month period, I had in fact been quoted more times than any other author, living or dead! Thus, the *Reader's Digest* has now given me good grounds for claiming to be the *World's Most Quotable Person.*[6]

Alphabet Gravy

This new honor comes in addition to the earlier one bestowed upon me by the Hallmark Card Company, which enabled me to claim the (still undisputed) title of World's Highest Paid Published Author (Per Word).[7] But even that sensational achievement pales somewhat into insignificance beside my newest claim to fame, which came about as the result of a case involving the registered trade-mark, POT-SHOTS,® which I have owned since 1970. Another card company came along which wanted very much to call their own "pop-up" cards POP-SHOTS.® Because of the similarity of spelling and sound, there was some possibility of confusion, which gave me good grounds for objecting. But, after considerable legal wrangling, an agreement was worked out whereby I withdrew my objection and received in return a total compensation of $10,000. Since the entire issue had hinged on the difference made by just one consonant, I can now claim to be not only the highest-paid author per word, but also probably the only one in history who ever got *$10,000 for a Single Letter of the Alphabet!*

Of Theme I Sing

Since each of this book's six predecessors has had twelve chapters, each chapter with its own theme, and since that arrangement has apparently had no dire consequences, my publisher has almost superstitiously insisted that we follow the same formula once again. On the question of an overall theme for the whole book, however, he has been a little more

[6]Here are the five Brilliant Thoughts which brought me this remarkable distinction, with the dates of their appearance in *Readers Digest*:

#3945: THE OLDER YOU GET, THE MORE IMPORTANT IT IS NOT TO ACT YOUR AGE. (March 1988)

#3191: THE BEST REASON FOR HAVING DREAMS IS THAT IN DREAMS NO REASONS ARE NECESSARY. (April 1988)

#3962: IF WE COULD ALL HEAR EACH OTHER'S PRAYERS, GOD MIGHT BE RELIEVED OF SOME OF HIS BURDEN. (July 1988)

#4254: SOMETIMES THE MOST URGENT AND VITAL THING YOU CAN POSSIBLY DO IS TAKE A COMPLETE REST. (January 1989)

#3317: IT'S NOT EASY TAKING MY PROBLEMS ONE AT A TIME, WHEN THEY REFUSE TO GET IN LINE. (April 1989)

[7]See Book V, p.10. It was this feat which inspired the title of my address to the Willamette Writers' Conference (Portland, Oregon, August 12, 1989): "HOW TO MAKE MORE BY WRITING LESS."

flexible. Twice before, we have tried such a device[8] without (so far as can be determined from the great dearth of comments received) any reader ever being aware of it.

But there must be *some* people who feel that a book should be *about* something, and in hopes of appeasing them, I have decided once again to have an official theme. Since the last book was more or less about TIME, this one will at least genuflect in the direction of SPACE, and in particular will concern itself with TRAVEL, as in traveling through life. If, however, just the thought of having a theme makes you scream, or if you tend to unravel at the very idea of travel, please remember that this new ingredient is supplied at no extra charge, and you are perfectly free once again to confound me by ignoring it.

Getting Somewhere

In my own personal life, the two themes of Travel and the Quest for Recognition have become increasingly intertwined. This was vividly demonstrated, for example, in the spring of 1988, when, at the behest of three diverse but compelling invitations, I found myself, within the space of a single month, first racing across the Arctic Circle to bring the gospel of POT-SHOTS® to Eskimo school-children living in the farthest northern settlement on this continent[9] then dashing South to dazzle American Booksellers at their Association's annual convention in Anaheim, California, then hastening East in order to share my illuminations with U.S. service men and women stationed in Germany (thereby also somehow helping to loosen the foundations of the celebrated Berlin Wall, which, as I predicted it would, collapsed soon thereafter)[10] The European portion of this journey was actually sanctified by an agency of the U.S. department of Defense, with an official declaration that my use of Government transportation and accommodation had been determined to be "in the best public interest." (See document, page 16.)

---

[8]Book IV: Health, and Book VI: The Calendar.

[9]After what may have been the first journey ever performed in a single day from Santa Barbara, California, to Barrow, on the north coast of Alaska.

[10]In choosing places to visit, I seem to have an uncanny ability to bring on spectacular events. In early 1981, I went to have a look at what were then the peaceful and practically unheard-of Falkland Islands and was scarcely home again before the amazing Falklands War between Britain and Argentina erupted. I was in the equally obscure (and equally peaceful) Soviet city of Baku not long before major disturbances there put Baku in everybody's headlines. And my ten days in remote and unknown Barrow, Alaska, were almost immediately followed by a dramatic incident, involving attempts to free some whales trapped there in the ice, which for days made Barrow a focus of world attention. (You may wish to consider these facts before inviting me to *your* community!)

DEPARTMENT OF DEFENSE
EUROPEAN STARS AND STRIPES
APO New York 09211

REPLY TO
ATTENTION OF

ECSS-EIC   23 May 1988

SUBJECT: Invitational Travel Orders

Mr. Ashleigh Brilliant
c/o MSgt. Barry R. Cantor
    Chief, Broadcast Operations
    AFN-Berlin
    APO 09742

1. Under the provisions of paragraph C6003, Volume 2, Joint Travel Regulations,
you are invited to proceed from Berlin in sufficient time to arrive at Frankfurt,
West Germany, 7 June 1988, for the purpose of AFNTV taping sessions on 7 June
and Stars and Stripes author promotions of your literary works on 8 and 9 June
1988. Upon completion of the mission you will return to your point of origin.

2. Travel to Frankfurt is authorized and arranged by AFN-Berlin. The use of
government billeting in the Frankfurt and Mission areas is authorized.

3. Address any inquiries regarding this travel order to the undersigned.

4. The travel and use of accomodations authorized through these orders have been
determined to be in the best public interest. Charges and expenses incurred by
you under these authorizations are not chargeable to the Stars and Stripes Fund.

FOR THE COMMANDER

                                    SUZANNE L. PHILLIPS
                                    Lieutenant Colonel, USAF
                                    Deputy/Commander/Editor in Chief

DISTRIBUTION:

5 - Individual Concerned
1 - Finance and Accounting Section
2 - Rec & Ref Set, CPO

This was highly gratifying to a humble foreign-born luminary like myself, whose whole career had sprung out of the counter-culture of the 1960's and who had once had to overcome ten years of official opposition to his efforts to become a U.S. citizen.[11]

Running to Seed

Not all of my journeys, however, have had to do with planting my thoughts about the world. Some have become involved with other kinds of cultivation. In 1986, for example, I grafted my personal endorsement upon the renowned "Peace Tree" planted some years before at Sochi, in the Soviet Union, with results which are still unfolding. My visit to pacific (and Atlantic) Costa Rica the following year was similarly motivated, and it was there that I took particular interest in the fruit of another kind of tree which I happened to try one day. It was called a Cherimoya, and I found it to be so ecstatically delectable that I became obsessed with a desire to proclaim my exciting discovery to a presumably ignorant world. I had visions of playing Sir Walter Raleigh, returning from the tropics and bringing back to my amazed compatriots the seeds of a new edible treasure. This juicy figment of my mind was, however, soon squashed after I got home, since it turned out that Cherimoyas were already well-known in California, and had in fact been grown locally for generations.

Fault Line

Naturally (and in the spirit of this book's title), I blamed my wife, who had been through so much with me on that trip and on many others, and who claims to be much more plant-wise than I am, for this embarrassment. But you and I, dear Reader, joined in our own hopefully fruitful bond, will also in these pages be going through quite a lot together. And, although I can't very easily blame *you* for every such occasion on which my wisdom may find itself, so to speak, with fruit on its face, I hope you realize that, if you keep enjoying these Brilliant Thoughts,® you really are largely responsible for my laborious task of continuing to nurture, harvest, and disseminate them. But that, I have to admit, is one of your more endearing faults.

[11]See Book I, p. 9.

POT-SHOTS NO. 4727.

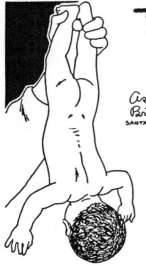

Ashleigh Brilliant
SANTA BARBARA

THERE'S ONE WAY
IN WHICH
MY LIFE
HASN'T
CHANGED
SINCE
I WAS BORN:

IT'S STILL
MY LIFE.

© ASHLEIGH BRILLIANT 1988.

Chapter I

Self Starter

If life is a journey, let's get started! On the other hand, let's not rush into anything. First we must choose a suitable mode of travel. For all-around convenience, let me suggest a handy vehicle called the Self. No matter whether you see your own life as a pilgrimage, a voyage of discovery, a crusade, or just an aimless wandering, the rugged human Self is probably your best bet for dependable transportation.

Selves are so numerous that they often clog the traffic-lanes of this world, yet each one encompasses its own apparently infinite universe of thoughts and feelings. With a luggage compartment full of memories and dreams, and a fuel-tank continually replenished with hope, the Self has almost everything anybody needs for a pleasant journey through time and space, except perhaps (in many cases) a known and comfortable destination.

This may not be your only guide-book for the trip, but, just in case it is, let me caution you at the outset to stay well within the vehicle at all times. And please, at this stage, resist any temptation to tinker with your own finely-tuned automatic controls, since it has not yet been established exactly which parts of the Self are user-serviceable.

In the unlikely event of an emergency, you may be glad you took the time to become familiar with the Self-oriented sentiments I have thoughtfully provided for you in the following guidelines.

POT-SHOTS NO. 4670.

THE WORLD ISN'T MAKING VERY GOOD USE OF ME ~

BUT
IS THAT
THE WORLD'S FAULT,
OR MINE?

©ASHLEIGH BRILLIANT 1988.

Ashleigh Brilliant
SANTA BARBARA

POT-SHOTS NO. 4354.

Ashleigh
Brilliant
SANTA BARBARA

I KNOW MY LIMITATIONS,

ONE
OF
WHICH
IS BEING
TOO
AMBITIOUS.

©ASHLEIGH BRILLIANT 1988.

POT-SHOTS NO. 4378.

WHAT YOU OWE TO YOURSELF

Ashleigh
Brilliant
SANTA BARBARA

CAN BE
VERY DIFFICULT
TO COLLECT.

©ASHLEIGH BRILLIANT 1988.

POT-SHOTS NO. 4600.

© ASHLEIGH BRILLIANT 1988.

WHICH DO I NEED MORE ~

TO PULL MYSELF TOGETHER,

OR TO LET MYSELF GO?

Ashleigh Brilliant
SANTA BARBARA

POT-SHOTS NO. 4622.

© ASHLEIGH BRILLIANT 1988.

I DON'T LIKE SITUATIONS IN WHICH, IF ANYTHING GOES WRONG, I HAVE ONLY MYSELF TO BLAME.

Ashleigh Brilliant
SANTA BARBARA

© ASHLEIGH BRILLIANT 1988.

POT-SHOTS NO. 4626.

I'D PROBABLY FUNCTION MUCH BETTER

IF SOMEBODY MORE QUALIFIED THAN I AM WERE IN CHARGE OF ME.

Ashleigh Brilliant
SANTA BARBARA

IT'S HARD ENOUGH TO BE ALIVE AND HUMAN,
WITHOUT THE ADDITIONAL BURDEN OF BEING ME.

WHY DO I SENSE DANGER,
WHENEVER I GET TOO CLOSE TO MYSELF?

IS THAT ALL I AM?
— JUST A RESULT OF SOMETHING THAT HAPPENED ONE DAY LONG AGO?

© ASHLEIGH BRILLIANT 1988.   POT-SHOTS NO. 4306.

I MIGHT VALUE MYSELF MORE HIGHLY,

IF I DIDN'T KNOW ME SO WELL.

Ashleigh Brilliant
SANTA BARBARA

© ASHLEIGH BRILLIANT 1989.   POT-SHOTS NO. 4854.

WHATEVER BECAME OF THE PERSON I WAS HOPING TO BECOME?

Ashleigh Brilliant
SANTA BARBARA

© ASHLEIGH BRILLIANT 1989.   POT-SHOTS NO. 4938.

ONE THING I'VE LEARNED FROM MY MISTAKES

IS HOW TO MAKE MISTAKES.

Ashleigh Brilliant
SANTA BARBARA

POT-SHOTS NO. 4634. ©ASHLEIGH BRILLIANT 1988.

HOW DISTRESSING!

I CAN'T REMEMBER WHETHER OR NOT I'M SATISFIED.

Ashleigh Brilliant
SANTA BARBARA

©ASHLEIGH BRILLIANT 1988   POT-SHOTS NO. 4709.

I KNOW I'M OFTEN UNAWARE ~

BUT AT LEAST I'M AWARE OF MY LACK OF AWARENESS.

Ashleigh Brilliant
SANTA BARBARA

©ASHLEIGH BRILLIANT 1988.   POT-SHOTS NO. 4716.

I'M PROUD OF THE FACT

THAT I SOMEHOW KEEP GOING WITH SO LITTLE TO BE PROUD OF.

Ashleigh Brilliant
SANTA BARBARA

POT-SHOTS NO. 4451.

IT'S GETTING HARDER AND HARDER,

BUT
SO FAR
I HAVE SURVIVED
EVERY
ENCOUNTER
WITH
MY MIRROR.

POT-SHOTS NO. 4462.

THERE ARE TIMES
WHEN
I WISH
SOMEBODY WHO
UNDERSTANDS ME
WOULD
TELL ME
WHAT
I MEAN.

Ashleigh
Brilliant
SANTA BARBARA

POT-SHOTS NO. 4459.

I AM TRYING VERY HARD TO FUNCTION

IN A
HOSTILE
ENVIRONMENT
CALLED "LIFE".

Ashleigh Brilliant
SANTA BARBARA

POT-SHOTS NO. 4774.

AT WHAT
STAGE
OF MY
LIFE CYCLE
AM I
SUPPOSED
TO
FIND
HAPPINESS?

©ASHLEIGH BRILLIANT 1988.

Ashleigh
Brilliant
SANTA BARBARA

©ASHLEIGH BRILLIANT 1988.

POT-SHOTS NO.4373.

I'VE NEVER HAD
A TOTAL FAILURE,

BUT
HAVE HAD
SOME
LEARNING
EXPERIENCES
I WOULDN'T
WANT TO
REPEAT.

Ashleigh Brilliant
SANTA BARBARA

©ASHLEIGH BRILLIANT 1989.

POT-SHOTS NO. 4858.

ONCE
I GET
STARTED,
NOTHING
CAN
STOP ME ~

BUT
SOMETIMES IT
SEEMS THAT
NOTHING
CAN START ME.

Ashleigh
Brilliant
SANTA BARBARA

© ASHLEIGH BRILLIANT 1989.

POT-SHOTS NO. 4935.

WHAT WOULD I BE, WITHOUT MY IDENTITY?

Ashleigh Brilliant
SANTA BARBARA.

© ASHLEIGH BRILLIANT 1985.

POT-SHOTS NO. 3575.

NO WONDER I KEEP STUMBLING ~

BOTH MY SHOES ARE FULL OF FEET,

Ashleigh Brilliant
SANTA BARBARA

© ASHLEIGH BRILLIANT 1989.

POT-SHOTS NO. 4876.

IT'S SURPRISING HOW MANY THINGS

DEPEND ON THE ANSWER TO THE QUESTION: WHERE AM I?

Ashleigh Brilliant
SANTA BARBARA

© ASHLEIGH BRILLIANT 1988.   Ashleigh Brilliant   POT-SHOTS NO. 4337.

WHAT'S
CONFUSING
ABOUT
MY
LIFE STORY

IS THAT
THE PLOT
BEGAN
BEFORE
I CAME
ON
THE SCENE.

Ashleigh Brilliant SANTA BARBARA

© ASHLEIGH BRILLIANT 1989.   POT-SHOTS NO. 5000.

I MUST
STAY
ALIVE
UNTIL
MY WORK
IS DONE ~
BUT AFTER THAT,
WHAT EXCUSE
WILL I HAVE?

Ashleigh Brilliant SANTA BARBARA

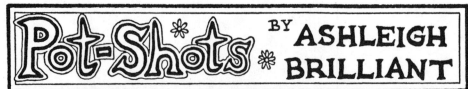
POT-SHOTS NO. 4329.

YOU'RE
THE
BEST THING
THAT'S
HAPPENED
TO ME
TODAY ~

BUT
IT'S EARLY YET.

Ashleigh Brilliant

SANTA BARBARA

Chapter II

Thee, We, and Me

Traveling along the trajectory of our lives, sooner or later we become aware of the occupants of other Selves, all of whom, by some linguistic quirk, answer to the name of "YOU," and most of whom seem to have a ridiculously exaggerated idea of their own importance compared with ours. No definitive work on how to deal with these creatures, who are always somehow at the other end of any one-on-one relationship, has yet been written. My own feeling has generally been that, purely in the interests of Science, I should scrutinize them as closely as circumstances permit, while trying to avoid any disturbance of their natural habitat. Unfortunately, however, I have found it impossible conscientiously to observe these curious beings without to some extent becoming involved with them.

Nevertheless, some of my best thoughts have resulted from persistent efforts to overcome the "you-me barrier" and communicate across the cosmic reaches of inter-personal space. Often the messages which have reached me from those distant regions have been hopelessly garbled. But there have been times when they have come through with astounding clarity, and so powerfully as to leave marks on the psyche, or even on the skin. Such possibilities should not, however, deter your own high-minded research, for the benefit of which the following Brilliant study-aids are solicitiously supplied.

POT-SHOTS NO. 4392.

I'LL NEVER
CHANGE
THE ENTIRE
WORLD,

SO
I MIGHT AS WELL
BEGIN BY
FAILING TO
CHANGE YOU.

Ashleigh Brilliant
SANTA BARBARA

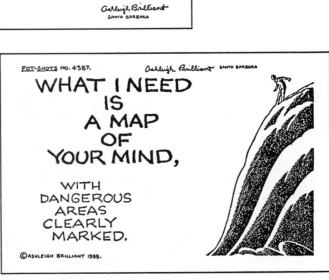

POT-SHOTS NO. 4387.   Ashleigh Brilliant   SANTA BARBARA

WHAT I NEED
IS
A MAP
OF
YOUR MIND,

WITH
DANGEROUS
AREAS
CLEARLY
MARKED.

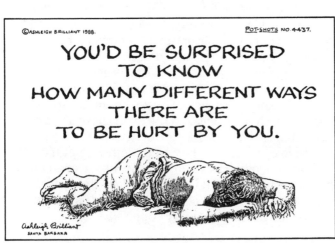

POT-SHOTS NO. 4437.

YOU'D BE SURPRISED
TO KNOW
HOW MANY DIFFERENT WAYS
THERE ARE
TO BE HURT BY YOU.

Ashleigh Brilliant
SANTA BARBARA

POT-SHOTS NO.4417   Ashleigh Brilliant   SANTA BARBARA

ALL I ASK IS THAT YOU CONTINUE INDEFINITELY TO LET ME TAKE ADVANTAGE OF YOUR GOOD NATURE.

©ASHLEIGH BRILLIANT 1988.

©ASHLEIGH BRILLIANT 1988.   POT-SHOTS NO. 4497.

FOR YOUR OWN SAFETY,

PLEASE STAY BEHIND THE LINE I HAVE DRAWN AROUND MY SUPPLY OF CHOCOLATE.

Ashleigh Brilliant
SANTA BARBARA

POT-SHOTS NO.4457.

DON'T FORGET! WE DON'T HAVE A DATE.

©ASHLEIGH BRILLIANT 1988.   Ashleigh Brilliant
SANTA BARBARA

POT-SHOTS NO. 4742. ©ASHLEIGH BRILLIANT 1988.

THE NEXT BEST THING TO HAPPINESS

IS UNHAPPINESS SHARED WITH YOU.

Ashleigh Brilliant SANTA BARBARA

©ASHLEIGH BRILLIANT 1988.

Ashleigh Brilliant SANTA BARBARA

POT-SHOTS NO. 4714.

I LIKE TO MAKE YOU LAUGH,

BECAUSE THEN I HAVE YOU HELPLESS, AND IN MY POWER.

©ASHLEIGH BRILLIANT 1988.

POT-SHOTS NO. 4712.

WHENEVER I'M ALONE WITH YOU,

WHY DO I ALWAYS FEEL OUTNUMBERED?

Ashleigh Brilliant SANTA BARBARA

HOW CAN I RESPECT YOUR JUDGMENT,

IF YOU TRUST PEOPLE LIKE ME?

Ashleigh Brilliant
SANTA BARBARA

ALL I ASK IS THAT ALL YOUR FUTURE BEHAVIOR BE COMPLETELY OUT OF CHARACTER.

Ashleigh Brilliant
SANTA BARBARA

DON'T HOLD YOUR BREATH UNTIL I IMPROVE ~

I DON'T WANT TO BE RESPONSIBLE FOR YOUR SUFFOCATION.

Ashleigh Brilliant
SANTA BARBARA

© ASHLEIGH BRILLIANT 1988. POT-SHOTS NO. 4760

WHY ARE MY MEMORIES OF THINGS WE DID TOGETHER

SO OFTEN SO DIFFERENT FROM YOURS?

Ashleigh Brilliant
SANTA BARBARA

© ASHLEIGH BRILLIANT 1988. POT-SHOTS NO. 4745.

Ashleigh Brilliant
SANTA BARBARA

IF YOU MUST CATCH ME OFF-GUARD,

LET IT BE WHEN I'M DOING SOMETHING RIGHT.

© ASHLEIGH BRILLIANT 1989. POT-SHOTS NO. 4787.

IF YOU DON'T LIKE HOW I SOUND,

THE TROUBLE MAY BE WITH HOW YOU'RE LISTENING.

Ashleigh Brilliant
SANTA BARBARA

© ASHLEIGH BRILLIANT 1988.

POT-SHOTS NO. 4769.

IF THE WHOLE WORLD'S ON MY SIDE, BUT YOU'RE AGAINST ME,

I HAVEN'T GOT A CHANCE.

Ashleigh Brilliant
SANTA BARBARA

© ASHLEIGH BRILLIANT 1988.

POT-SHOTS NO. 4653.

AREN'T WE LUCKY THERE ARE SO MANY THINGS ABOUT EACH OTHER THAT WE DON'T ENVY!

Ashleigh Brilliant
SANTA BARBARA

© ASHLEIGH BRILLIANT 1989.

POT-SHOTS NO. 4881.

I MADE A MISTAKE

IN NOT TELLING YOU SOONER THAT I AM INFALLIBLE.

Ashleigh Brilliant
SANTA BARBARA

Thee, We, and Me 37

POT-SHOTS NO. 4829

Isn't there any way I can persuade you to abandon your fundamental principles of decency?

©ASHLEIGH BRILLIANT 1989.

©ASHLEIGH BRILLIANT 1988.

POT-SHOTS NO. 4773.

UNTIL I MET YOU,

I THOUGHT THE WORLD HAD SOME RATIONAL BASIS.

Ashleigh Brilliant
SANTA BARBARA

©ASHLEIGH BRILLIANT 1989.

POT-SHOTS NO. 4882.

NO! NO!

FOR GOD'S SAKE, DON'T USE YOUR OWN BEST JUDGMENT!

Ashleigh Brilliant
SANTA BARBARA

© ASHLEIGH BRILLIANT 1988.

POT-SHOTS NO. 4449.

DON'T EXPECT MIRACLES FROM ME,

UNLESS YOU'RE PREPARED TO PAY THE CURRENT HIGH PRICE OF MIRACLES.

Ashleigh Brilliant
SANTA BARBARA

© ASHLEIGH BRILLIANT 1989

POT-SHOTS NO. 4914.

DO YOU BELIEVE IN APATHY AT FIRST SIGHT?

Ashleigh Brilliant
SANTA BARBARA

© ASHLEIGH BRILLIANT 1989.

POT-SHOTS NO. 4977.

FORGIVE ME

FOR FINDING IT IMPOSSIBLE TO FORGIVE YOU.

Ashleigh Brilliant
SANTA BARBARA

Thee, We, and Me **39**

© ASHLEIGH BRILLIANT 1989.　POT-SHOTS NO. 4892.

YOU ARE THE ANSWER

to several problems
I didnt even know
I had,
until
I met you.

© ASHLEIGH BRILLIANT 1988.　POT-SHOTS NO. 4355.

IF I HAD ONLY ONE MORE MISTAKE TO MAKE,

I WOULD
WANT TO
MAKE IT
WITH YOU.

© ASHLEIGH BRILLIANT 1989.　POT-SHOTS NO. 4917.

AT LEAST I'VE CONVINCED YOU TO MY OWN SATISFACTION.

© ASHLEIGH BRILLIANT 1989.

POT-SHOTS NO.4933.

I'M GLAD OUR FRIENDSHIP WAS YOUR IDEA,

BECAUSE I MIGHT NEVER HAVE THOUGHT OF IT.

© ASHLEIGH BRILLIANT 1989.

POT-SHOTS NO.4984.

WE ARE UNITED IN OUR DETERMINATION

TO GO OUR SEPARATE WAYS.

Pot-Shots

BY ASHLEIGH BRILLIANT

POT-SHOTS NO. 4346.

I'M SORRY
PEOPLE
DON'T ALWAYS
KEEP THEIR
PROMISES,

BUT GLAD
THEY DON'T
ALWAYS
CARRY OUT
THEIR
THREATS.

Ashleigh Brilliant
SANTA BARBARA

Chapter III

Human Nature Trail

No life traveler ever gets very far, at least not in this part of the galaxy, before coming upon an obstacle called "People," a beast whose quirky behavior patterns (often ascribed to a mysterious force known as Human Nature), will form the focus of this chapter.

Few dilemmas of daily life are more vexing than that of having to cope with Humanity while at the same time finding oneself to be a part of it. Considering how many of us are preoccupied with this task, it surprises me that no courses are offered in the subject at any of our institutions of learning.

Hoping to remedy this deficiency, I did once somehow convince the administrators of our local "Continuing Education" program to let me teach a 12-week course which I called "HOW TO BE WHAT YOU ARE." (Santa Barbara City College, Fall 1974). The lesson titles were all Brilliant Thoughts® such as "TOMORROW IS ANOTHER DAY TO WASTE" (#134) and "JUST WHEN I NEARLY HAD THE ANSWER, I FORGOT THE QUESTION" (#216), and the course description promised, among other things, a series of "rambling monologues" by the instructor on such topics as "The Fallacy of Human Dignity" and "How to Overcome Ambition." The extent of my success may be judged by the fact that, by the end of the course, the overwhelming majority of my students were actually unchanged in any way whatsoever. And even today, after all the intervening years, when I happen to re-meet them, I am proud to see that some of those same students are still being what they are.

© ASHLEIGH BRILLIANT 1988.

POT-SHOTS NO. 4341.

BEING HUMBLE

IS WITH ME A MATTER OF GREAT PRIDE.

Ashleigh Brilliant
SANTA BARBARA

© ASHLEIGH BRILLIANT 1988.

POT-SHOTS NO. 4425.

Ashleigh Brilliant
SANTA BARBARA

WHY ARE THERE ALWAYS SO MANY OPPORTUNITIES FOR ME TO PUT MY SHYNESS ON PUBLIC DISPLAY?

© ASHLEIGH BRILLIANT 1988.

POT-SHOTS NO. 4423.

I'VE DISCOVERED MORE WAYS I'M RIGHT AND YOU'RE WRONG ~ AREN'T YOU ANXIOUS TO HEAR THEM?

Ashleigh Brilliant SANTA BARBARA

© ASHLEIGH BRILLIANT 1988. POT-SHOTS NO. 4418.

SUPERSTITION ISN'T ALWAYS NECESSARY~

SOME MAGIC CHARMS BRING GOOD LUCK, WHETHER YOU BELIEVE IN THEM OR NOT.

Ashleigh Brilliant
SANTA BARBARA

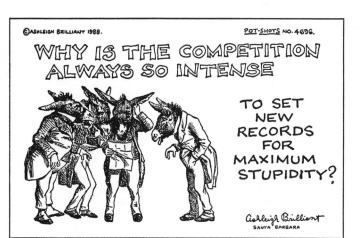

© ASHLEIGH BRILLIANT 1988. POT-SHOTS NO. 4696.

WHY IS THE COMPETITION ALWAYS SO INTENSE

TO SET NEW RECORDS FOR MAXIMUM STUPIDITY?

Ashleigh Brilliant
SANTA BARBARA

© ASHLEIGH BRILLIANT 1988. POT-SHOTS NO. 4411.

GREAT MINDS FORGET GREAT THINGS.

Ashleigh Brilliant
SANTA BARBARA

ONLY SHYNESS

PREVENTS SOME PEOPLE FROM BEING TOTALLY OBNOXIOUS.

© ASHLEIGH BRILLIANT 1988.

Ashleigh Brilliant
SANTA BARBARA

© ASHLEIGH BRILLIANT 1988.

YOU CAN CAUSE ACUTE DISCOMFORT

BY TRYING TOO HARD TO MAKE YOUR GUEST FEEL AT HOME.

Ashleigh Brilliant
SANTA BARBARA

PLEASE DON'T TELL ME THERE'S NO NEED TO WORRY ~

IT'S THE ONLY THING I'M ANY GOOD AT.

© ASHLEIGH BRILLIANT 1988

Ashleigh Brilliant
SANTA BARBARA

© ASHLEIGH BRILLIANT 1988. Ashleigh Brilliant SANTA BARBARA

POT-SHOTS NO. 4655.

SURELY YOU DON'T EXPECT AN HONEST ANSWER, WHEN YOUR QUESTION EXPOSES THE WEAKNESS OF MY ENTIRE POSITION.

© ASHLEIGH BRILLIANT 1988. Ashleigh Brilliant SANTA BARBARA

POT-SHOTS NO. 4735.

THE ONLY THING WORSE THAN BEING TOTALLY DEAD IS BEING SLIGHTLY OUT OF FASHION.

© ASHLEIGH BRILLIANT 1988.

POT-SHOTS NO. 4588.

WHAT LAW CAN MAKE THE BEAUTIFUL UGLY, AND THE UGLY BEAUTIFUL?

— THE LAW OF FASHION.

Ashleigh Brilliant SANTA BARBARA

©ASHLEIGH BRILLIANT 1988.   POT-SHOTS NO. 4679.

WHEN IT'S A CHOICE BETWEEN DISAPPOINTING ME AND TELLING LIES,

WHY DON'T YOU EVER TELL ME LIES?

©ASHLEIGH BRILLIANT 1989.   POT-SHOTS NO. 4334.

SPECIAL OFFER:

BUY ONE FOR TWICE THE PRICE, AND GET ANOTHER ONE FREE!

©ASHLEIGH BRILLIANT 1989.   POT-SHOTS NO. 4835.

SHOWING HOW MUCH YOU WANT IT

MAY OR MAY NOT HELP YOU GET IT.

POT-SHOTS NO. 4855. ©ASHLEIGH BRILLIANT 1989.

SOME PEOPLE SHOULD BE REQUIRED TO WEAR WARNING-SIGNS.

DANGER

Ashleigh Brilliant
SANTA BARBARA

POT-SHOTS
NO. 4737.

YES, BUT ACCEPTING RESPONSIBILITY FOR MY OWN PROBLEMS WOULD PUT ME IN A VERY WEAK BARGAINING POSITION.

©ASHLEIGH BRILLIANT 1988.

Ashleigh Brilliant
SANTA BARBARA

©ASHLEIGH BRILLIANT 1988.

POT-SHOTS
NO. 4554.

Ashleigh Brilliant
SANTA BARBARA

ALL I NEED FOR A HAPPY LIFE

IS NEVER TO KNOW THE POSSIBILITY OF ANYTHING BETTER.

I ENJOY DOING THINGS ON THE SPUR OF THE MOMENT,

PROVIDED I'M GIVEN AMPLE TIME TO PREPARE.

© ASHLEIGH BRILLIANT 1989.

POT-SHOTS NO. 4956.

© ASHLEIGH BRILLIANT 1989.

POT-SHOTS NO. 4847.

FOREIGNERS SHOULD BE PREVENTED FROM COMING TO OUR COUNTRY,

AND DOING WHAT WE'VE ALWAYS DONE IN THEIRS.

© ASHLEIGH BRILLIANT 1988.

POT-SHOTS NO. 4435.

NO WONDER MY NEW IDEA SEEMED SO GREAT~

IT'S THE SAME ONE I HAD TWENTY YEARS AGO.

© ASHLEIGH BRILLIANT 1988.

POT-SHOTS NO. 4416.

PEOPLE WHO NEED TO RECEIVE CARE

ARE USEFUL AND NECESSARY TO PEOPLE WHO NEED TO GIVE IT.

Ashleigh Brilliant
SANTA BARBARA

POT-SHOTS NO. 4363.

ANYBODY CAN BE WRONG OCCASIONALLY,

Ashleigh Brilliant
SANTA BARBARA

BUT ONLY TRULY EXCEPTIONAL PEOPLE CAN MAKE AN ENTIRE CAREER OF IT.

© ASHLEIGH BRILLIANT 1988

POT-SHOTS NO. 3850.

WE MAY BE RELATED IN SOME WAY,

BUT I DON'T NECESSARILY HOLD THAT AGAINST YOU.

Ashleigh
Brilliant
SANTA BARBARA

Chapter IV

Familiar Terms

The landscape of our lives is dotted with odd formations in the shape of relatives, lovers, and various other intimates, all of whose close claims upon us form part of a vaguely intimidating panorama. These strange configurations may appear quite foreign and foreboding to the anxious traveler who goes racing past them in the night, perceiving only the dark outlines of complex relationships, with here and there the light of a burning romance or a radiant friendship piercing the gloom. But this is actually the wierd world of everyday experience, and in the dawn it can, for each one of us, begin to take on a bewilderingly familiar aspect.

The well-known phenomenon that people appear to become more peculiar as we get closer to them may be something more than a mere optical illusion. In the final analysis, our most natural role in life may really be that of the stranger, which, after all, is the condition in which we were born into this world (as your mother will verify), and in which we will presumably enter any subsequent reality. Those persons must truly be exceptional who have never felt at least slightly extraneous in their own households, in the unsettling company of their own kith and kin. Indeed, as the following messages may demonstrate, it is often about our nearest and dearest that our minds tend to be unclearest.

BE ON GUARD!

SOMEWHERE AT LOOSE IN THE NEIGHBORHOOD IS AN ESCAPED HUSBAND.

Ashleigh Brilliant
SANTA BARBARA

Ashleigh Brilliant
SANTA BARBARA

I wish relationships could be tested in advance for safety, comfort, and durability.

AS LONG AS THERE ARE CHILDREN IN THE WORLD,

Ashleigh Brilliant
SANTA BARBARA

THERE WILL NEVER BE ANY REAL PEACE.

POT-SHOTS NO. 4512.

WHEN
I TIRE
OF AN
UNPLEASANT
TASK,

THERE ARE
ALWAYS
OTHER
UNPLEASANT
TASKS
I CAN
TURN TO.

Ashleigh Brilliant
SANTA BARBARA

POT-SHOTS NO. 4485.

HOPES ARE DIMMING
IN THE SEARCH
FOR
INTELLIGENT
LIFE
IN MY
FAMILY.

Ashleigh Brilliant
SANTA BARBARA

POT-SHOTS NO. 4532.

THINK
BIG,

AND REMEMBER
THAT NOTHING
IS BIGGER
THAN LOVE.

Ashleigh Brilliant
SANTA BARBARA

POT-SHOTS NO. 4475.

ONE THING YOU CAN LEARN BY ASKING QUESTIONS

IS THAT
SOMETIMES
IT'S BEST
NOT TO
ASK QUESTIONS.

©ASHLEIGH BRILLIANT 1988.

Ashleigh Brilliant
SANTA BARBARA

©ASHLEIGH BRILLIANT 1988.

POT-SHOTS NO. 4551.

Despite all
modern safeguards,

many marriages
continue to be
the result
of
human error.

Ashleigh Brilliant
SANTA BARBARA

POT-SHOTS NO. 4489.

I LOVE MY FAMILY,

AND
WOULD DO
ANYTHING
TO KEEP THEM
FROM HURTING ME.

©ASHLEIGH BRILLIANT 1988

Ashleigh Brilliant
SANTA BARBARA

© ASHLEIGH BRILLIANT 1988. POT-SHOTS NO. 4571.

Ashleigh Brilliant SANTA BARBARA

LOVE IS A VERY POWERFUL MEDICINE,

IF YOU CAN ENDURE SOME OF THE SIDE-EFFECTS.

© ASHLEIGH BRILLIANT 1988. POT-SHOTS NO. 4612.

ISN'T IT LUCKY
that what we want
from each other

nobody else
wants
from
either of us!

Ashleigh Brilliant SANTA BARBARA

© ASHLEIGH BRILLIANT 1988. POT-SHOTS NO. 4581.

You'd be
surprised
how many
things
I wouldn't
tolerate,

If I didn't
love you.

Ashleigh Brilliant SANTA BARBARA

© ASHLEIGH BRILLIANT 1988.

POT-SHOTS NO. 4668.

REGARDLESS OF THE SUBJECT,

SAYING THAT YOU LOVE ME IS NEVER TOTALLY IRRELEVANT.

© ASHLEIGH BRILLIANT 1988.

POT-SHOTS NO. 4643.

SOMETIMES IT'S HARD TO REMEMBER WHY I LOVE YOU,

CAN YOU GIVE ME A HINT?

© ASHLEIGH BRILLIANT 1988.

POT-SHOTS NO. 4683.

WHEN IN-LAWS ARE OUTLAWED,

ONLY OUTLAWS WILL HAVE IN-LAWS.

© ASHLEIGH BRILLIANT 1988. POT-SHOTS NO. 4694.

WE GAVE OUR CHILDREN EVERYTHING ~

WHEN WILL WE GET IT ALL BACK?

© ASHLEIGH BRILLIANT 1989. POT-SHOTS NO. 4942.

WANTED:

A PORTABLE ELECTRIC LOVER,

WITH A RE-CHARGEABLE HEART.

© ASHLEIGH BRILLIANT 1989. POT-SHOTS NO. 4867.

I WROTE YOUR NAME ON A FLOWER,

BUT IT DIED ANYWAY.

© ASHLEIGH BRILLIANT 1989. POT-SHOTS NO. 4811.

NOBODY EVER COMES OUT OF A SUCCESSFUL MARRIAGE VOLUNTARILY.

Ashleigh Brilliant SANTA BARBARA

© ASHLEIGH BRILLIANT 1989 POT-SHOTS NO. 4846.

IF SOME NEW LOVE DOESN'T ARRIVE SOON, I MAY HAVE TO DIP INTO MY RESERVE SUPPLY.

Ashleigh Brilliant SANTA BARBARA

© ASHLEIGH BRILLIANT 1989. POT-SHOTS NO. 4921.

THE BEST WAY TO BE A PRODUCTIVE CITIZEN IS NOT NECESSARILY BY PRODUCING MORE CITIZENS.

Ashleigh Brilliant SANTA BARBARA

© ASHLEIGH BRILLIANT 1988.

POT-SHOTS NO. 4649.

WHY DO SO MANY OF THE THINGS I LOVE HAVE TO BE PROTECTED FROM EACH OTHER?

Ashleigh Brilliant
SANTA BARBARA

© ASHLEIGH BRILLIANT 1989.

POT-SHOTS NO. 4792.

PLEASE LET ME KNOW,

IF YOU HAVE ANY LOVE THAT'S GOING TO WASTE.

Ashleigh Brilliant
SANTA BARBARA

© ASHLEIGH BRILLIANT 1988.

POT-SHOTS NO. 4654.

ADULTS KNOW MORE ABOUT BEING CHILDREN THAN CHILDREN KNOW ABOUT BEING ADULTS.

Ashleigh Brilliant
SANTA BARBARA

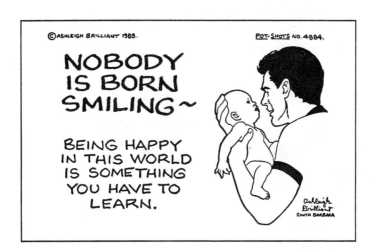

POT-SHOTS NO. 4875.

WHY
AM I
SO OFTEN
AT THE
MERCY
OF
THOSE WHO
DON'T
DESERVE
TO CONTROL MY LIFE?

Ashleigh Brilliant
SANTA BARBARA

Chapter V

Inter Play

Getting anywhere at all on the ocean of life calls for a complicated kind of navigation known as Human Relations. The hazards to be faced, as charted in the following pages, may be as large as an armada of friends and neighbors, or as small as a single spouse. Regardless of your plans, it always helps to know your position (if you have one), and to be aware of which way the wind is blowing.

People have of course been relating to each other for thousands of years, but for some reason, that does not seem to have made it any easier to do. Over the ages, various "Golden Rules" have been proposed (including the one that says, "Whoever has the Gold makes the Rules"), but we have not yet eliminated all conflicts, possibly because of pressure from novelists and dramatists, who would otherwise have nothing left to write about.

On the other hand, and in view of all our differences, we probably deserve some credit as a species just for tolerating each other as much as we do, particularly within such stressful settings as the typical family, where, even in the absence of a written constitution, internal business is nevertheless usually conducted without actual bloodshed.

Obviously it is not only laws and armaments which keep us from each other's throats. Deep down in every one of us there may lurk a sneaking suspicion that we are indeed all somehow part of one big family. But if this idea does not appeal to you, I hope that, in suggesting it, I have not totally ruined your day.

© ASHLEIGH BRILLIANT 1988.

POT-SHOTS NO. 4386.

WHAT IS THE BEST WAY TO FIGHT BACK

AGAINST ALL THE PEOPLE WHO ANNOY ME UNINTENTIONALLY?

Ashleigh Brilliant
SANTA BARBARA

© ASHLEIGH BRILLIANT 1988.

POT-SHOTS NO. 4530.

I DON'T LIKE TO OFFEND PEOPLE,

AND HOPE NOBODY FEELS OFFENDED BY THE FACT THAT I'M ALIVE.

Ashleigh Brilliant
SANTA BARBARA

© ASHLEIGH BRILLIANT 1988.

POT-SHOTS NO. 4439.

THE ONLY THING I DON'T LIKE ABOUT SOME PEOPLE

IS THE FACT THAT THEY DON'T LIKE ME.

Ashleigh Brilliant
SANTA BARBARA

© ASHLEIGH BRILLIANT 1989.

POT-SHOTS NO. 4872.

A BROKEN RELATIONSHIP CAN BE LIKE A SEVERED LIMB

~ YOU STILL FEEL IT, EVEN WHEN IT'S GONE.

Ashleigh Brilliant
SANTA BARBARA

WHY DO PEOPLE CARE SO MUCH MORE ABOUT HOW I BEHAVE

THAN ABOUT HOW I FEEL?

© ASHLEIGH BRILLIANT 1988.

POT-SHOTS NO. 4718.

Ashleigh Brilliant
SANTA BARBARA

© ASHLEIGH BRILLIANT 1988.

POT-SHOTS NO. 4434.

IT'S BEST TO LOVE SOME PEOPLE

AT A SAFE DISTANCE.

Ashleigh Brilliant
SANTA BARBARA

POT-SHOTS NO. 4960.

IF MY FRIENDS CAN TOLERATE ME,

WHY
CAN'T
MY
ENEMIES?

Ashleigh Brilliant
SANTA BARBARA

POT-SHOTS NO. 4913.

I BEG YOU TO TAKE ME WITH YOU ~

BUT
ONLY IF
I CAN BE
IN COMMAND.

Ashleigh
Brilliant
SANTA BARBARA

POT-SHOTS NO. 4538.

WHAT BINDS US MOST STRONGLY TOGETHER

IS
OUR LONG HISTORY
OF CONFLICT
WITH EACH OTHER.

Ashleigh
Brilliant
SANTA BARBARA

© ASHLEIGH BRILLIANT 1989.

POT-SHOTS NO. 4500.

MY RIDICULE IS FREE,

BUT
THERE WILL BE
A SLIGHT CHARGE
FOR MY
SYMPATHY.

Ashleigh Brilliant
SANTA BARBARA

© ASHLEIGH BRILLIANT 1989.

POT-SHOTS NO. 4544.

PLEASE PUT YOUR POVERTY AWAY ~

IT'S
MAKING
ME
TOO SAD.

Ashleigh Brilliant
SANTA BARBARA

© ASHLEIGH BRILLIANT 1989.

POT-SHOTS NO. 4784.

MEN AND WOMEN ARE SO DIFFERENT ~

WHATEVER
MADE GOD
THINK
THEY COULD
LIVE HAPPILY
TOGETHER?

Ashleigh Brilliant
SANTA BARBARA

WHY DO I KEEP CHANGING MY PLANS?

— BECAUSE IT'S USUALLY MUCH EASIER THAN CHANGING OTHER PEOPLE'S PLANS.

POT-SHOTS NO. 4580

© ASHLEIGH BRILLIANT 1988.

Ashleigh Brilliant
SANTA BARBARA

WOMEN CAN DO ANYTHING MEN CAN DO,

BUT OFTEN HAVE MORE SENSE THAN EVEN TO BE INTERESTED.

POT-SHOTS NO. 4366.

© ASHLEIGH BRILLIANT 1988.

Ashleigh Brilliant
SANTA BARBARA

THE ONLY WAY I CAN THINK OF TO THANK YOU FOR YOUR HELP

IS TO REQUEST MORE.

© ASHLEIGH BRILLIANT 1989. SANTA BARBARA.

POT-SHOTS NO. 4361.

Ashleigh Brilliant

© ASHLEIGH BRILLIANT 1989.

POT-SHOTS NO. 4972.

FINDERS AND WINNERS

BOTH NEED LOSERS.

Ashleigh Brilliant
SANTA BARBARA

© ASHLEIGH BRILLIANT 1988.

POT-SHOTS NO. 4749.

THE ONLY WAY FOR SOME NEIGHBORS TO LIVE IN PEACE

IS TO STOP BEING NEIGHBORS.

Ashleigh Brilliant
SANTA BARBARA

© ASHLEIGH BRILLIANT 1988.   POT-SHOTS NO. 4550.

Ashleigh
Brilliant
SANTA BARBARA

WHY
DOESN'T
THE WORLD
MAKE
MORE
OF AN
EFFORT
TO
UNDERSTAND
ME?

Chapter VI

World of Difference

We now come to the affairs of what is known as The World —
a place which has always been one of the chief repositories of
major natural resources, and which once used to be a popular
attraction for travelers. Most parts of it are reached today by a
means which is still called "travel" — a word significantly
derived from "travail" — but which has now become a mere
commodity dispensed in the form of little tour-packages by
"travel-agents," and which no longer bears much resemblance
to the truly meaningful type of experience we associate with
Traveling Through Life.

Those who go forth into the world today as packaged tour-
ists, although they may like to feel adventurous, generally
face the prospect of nothing more daunting than a surly hotel
clerk, their chances of any real excitement, such as a terrorist
attack, being quite slim. I myself must admit that, in the
course of time, danger and discomfort have, for me, lost much
of their charm. Despite the lack of hardships, however, my own
passage through life has happily not so far been so tedious as
to induce me to turn back. And its frequent detours have at
least enabled me to capture and affix for you, in the album of
my mind, the following fuzzy glimpses of world affairs.

© ASHLEIGH BRILLIANT 1988.   POT-SHOTS NO. 4758.

TRAFFIC IS MOVING AT A STEADY RATE

OF ZERO KILOMETERS PER HOUR.

© ASHLEIGH BRILLIANT 1988.   POT-SHOTS NO. 4360.

HOW DO ANIMALS CONDUCT ALL THEIR AFFAIRS,

WITHOUT EVER SIGNING CONTRACTS, MAKING WILLS, OR PAYING TAXES?

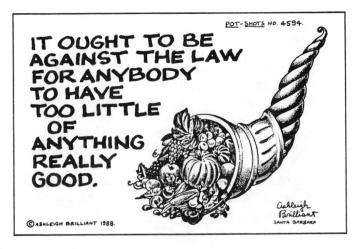

POT-SHOTS NO. 4594.

IT OUGHT TO BE AGAINST THE LAW FOR ANYBODY TO HAVE TOO LITTLE OF ANYTHING REALLY GOOD.

© ASHLEIGH BRILLIANT 1988.

POT-SHOTS NO. 4398.

IF
I MUST BE
HOMELESS,

I WOULD
PREFER
TO BE
HOMELESS
ONLY IN
THE DAYTIME.

©ASHLEIGH BRILLIANT 1988.

Ashleigh Brilliant
SANTA BARBARA

©ASHLEIGH BRILLIANT 1988.

POT-SHOTS NO. 4481.

THE
REWARDS
FOR
BREAKING
THE
RULES

CAN SOMETIMES
BE GREATER THAN
THE PENALTIES.

Ashleigh Brilliant
SANTA BARBARA

©ASHLEIGH BRILLIANT 1988.

POT-SHOTS NO. 4498.

THE MAJORITY
IS NEVER RIGHT,

UNLESS
IT
INCLUDES
ME.

Ashleigh Brilliant
SANTA BARBARA

GOOD PREVENTERS

NEVER KNOW
JUST HOW MANY
BAD THINGS
THEY
MAY HAVE
PREVENTED.

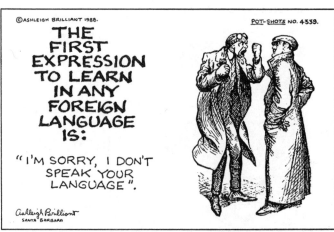

THE
FIRST
EXPRESSION
TO LEARN
IN ANY
FOREIGN
LANGUAGE
IS:

"I'M SORRY, I DON'T
SPEAK YOUR
LANGUAGE".

WHEN
EVERYONE
IS
GUILTY,
IT BECOMES
A CRIME TO BE INNOCENT.

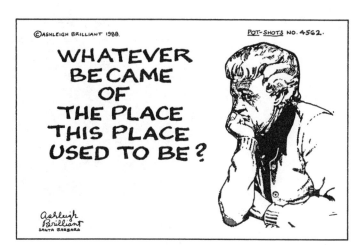

© ASHLEIGH BRILLIANT 1988.   POT-SHOTS NO. 4562.

WHATEVER
BECAME
OF
THE PLACE
THIS PLACE
USED TO BE?

Ashleigh
Brilliant
SANTA BARBARA

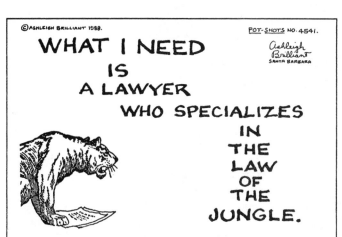

© ASHLEIGH BRILLIANT 1988.   POT-SHOTS NO. 4541.

WHAT I NEED
IS
A LAWYER
WHO SPECIALIZES
IN
THE
LAW
OF
THE
JUNGLE.

Ashleigh
Brilliant
SANTA BARBARA

© ASHLEIGH BRILLIANT 1988.   POT-SHOTS NO. 4568.

BEING DEAD
IS ONE WAY
TO EXPERIENCE
NOTHING~

ANOTHER
IS TO
ATTEND
SOME
CLASSES
AT MY
SCHOOL.

Ashleigh
Brilliant
SANTA BARBARA

© ASHLEIGH BRILLIANT 1988. Ashleigh Brilliant SANTA BARBARA POT-SHOTS NO. 4723.

HOW CAN SO MANY PEOPLE BE SO SHORT OF SPACE, WHEN THE UNIVERSE HAS SO MUCH OF IT?

© ASHLEIGH BRILLIANT 1988. POT-SHOTS NO. 4752.

HOW CAN WE LOVE OUR COUNTRY,

Ashleigh Brilliant SANTA BARBARA

UNLESS IT HAS THE POWER TO DESTROY THE WHOLE WORLD?

© ASHLEIGH BRILLIANT 1988. POT-SHOTS NO. 4615.

Ashleigh Brilliant SANTA BARBARA

WE FIND THE ACCUSED NOT ENTIRELY INNOCENT.

© ASHLEIGH BRILLIANT 1989. POT-SHOTS NO. 4837.

THEY OUGHT TO CENSOR EVERYDAY LIFE ~

IT'S BECOMING TOO SHOCKING.

Ashleigh Brilliant
SANTA BARBARA

© ASHLEIGH BRILLIANT 1988. POT-SHOTS NO. 4632.

WE OWE IT TO OUR PAST FUTILE SACRIFICES

TO CONTINUE MAKING FURTHER FUTILE SACRIFICES.

Ashleigh Brilliant
SANTA BARBARA

Ashleigh Brilliant
SANTA BARBARA

© ASHLEIGH BRILLIANT 1988. POT-SHOTS NO. 4624.

It's surprising how many questions there are to which the answer is: Money.

© ASHLEIGH BRILLIANT 1989. POT-SHOTS NO. 4878.

NO COUNTRY IS TRULY FREE,

WHERE THE CHILDREN ARE COMPELLED TO GO TO SCHOOL.

Ashleigh Brilliant
SANTA BARBARA

© ASHLEIGH BRILLIANT 1989. POT-SHOTS NO. 4947.

OPTIMISTIC ECOLOGISTS

ARE A VANISHING SPECIES.

Ashleigh Brilliant
SANTA BARBARA

© ASHLEIGH BRILLIANT 1989. POT-SHOTS NO. 4326.

VOTE WISELY,

Ashleigh Brilliant
SANTA BARBARA

EVEN IF THAT MEANS NOT VOTING AT ALL.

© ASHLEIGH BRILLIANT 1989. POT-SHOTS NO. 4901.

INCREDIBLE AS IT SEEMS, HALF OF ALL PEOPLE ARE LESS INTELLIGENT THAN THE AVERAGE PERSON.

POT-SHOTS NO. 4733.

BENEATH ALL THE WORLD'S TURMOIL, THERE'S A SECRET UNDERGROUND OF NORMAL PEOPLE LEADING NORMAL LIVES.

© ASHLEIGH BRILLIANT 1988.

© ASHLEIGH BRILLIANT 1989. POT-SHOTS NO. 4904.

WHAT WILL HAPPEN WHEN WORLD UNEMPLOYMENT REACHES 100%?

Pot-Shots BY ASHLEIGH BRILLIANT

Ashleigh Brilliant
SANTA BARBARA

POT-SHOTS
No. 4401.

I'D LIKE
TO
BELIEVE

THERE'S SOMETHING
BETTER
AT THE END
OF THIS LIFE ~

~ OR TO NOT CARE.

© ASHLEIGH BRILLIANT 1987.

Chapter VII

Life and the Other Thing

The time has come for me to introduce you to two of our fellow-passengers on this journey — Life and Death. Despite surface differences, the more you look at them, the harder they are to tell apart. They even have a trick of sometimes appearing actually to blend into one another, which can be quite mystifying. So here are a few clues to help you distinguish between them:

Of the two, Life is the only one you can lay down, lose, run for, take in your hands, escape with, or have the time of.

Death is the only one you can be bored to, snatched from the brink of, work yourself to, or be tickled to.

Life has its own cycle, its own boat, and its own magazine.

Death has its own bed, rattle, and valley.

Death is what used to part marriage partners, before divorce was invented. It is also what you are supposed to prefer to dishonor, but public opinion is gradually shifting in favor of dishonor.

Life (for some reason) tends to be of more interest to scientists, and Death to poets.

Death is what you really insure against when you buy Life Insurance.

As a final test — (if you can find the necessary aged canine upon which to perform it) — Life (as opposed to the other thing) is what you will find there is still some left of in the old dog yet.

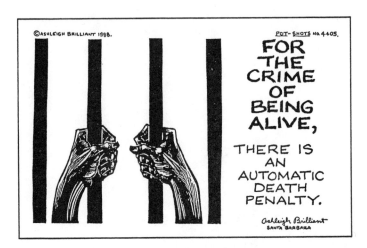

POT-SHOTS No. 4405.

FOR THE CRIME OF BEING ALIVE,

THERE IS AN AUTOMATIC DEATH PENALTY.

© ASHLEIGH BRILLIANT 1988.

Ashleigh Brilliant
SANTA BARBARA

POT-SHOTS No. 4342.

SOME GET MORE THAN THEY DESERVE,

OTHERS LESS ~

SO, AT LEAST ON AVERAGE, THE WORLD'S PERFECTLY FAIR.

Ashleigh Brilliant
SANTA BARBARA

© ASHLEIGH BRILLIANT 1988.

© ASHLEIGH BRILLIANT 1988.

POT-SHOTS No. 4432.

MY SCHEDULE IS FAST FILLING UP

WITH EMPTY DAYS.

Ashleigh Brilliant
SANTA BARBARA

THE CHANCES OF EVENTUAL DEATH ARE CURRENTLY 100% ~

THAT DOES NOT SEEM LIKE VERY SPORTING ODDS.

POT-SHOTS NO. 4455.

© ASHLEIGH BRILLIANT 1988.

© ASHLEIGH BRILLIANT 1988.

POT-SHOTS NO. 4394.

THE PENALTY OF SURVIVING

IS THAT YOU LOSE TOUCH WITH THOSE WHO DON'T SURVIVE.

Ashleigh Brilliant
SANTA BARBARA

POT-SHOTS NO. 4469.

SOMETHING'S WRONG WITH MY LIFE ~

SHOULD I TRY TO FIX IT, OR WAIT UNTIL I GET ANOTHER?

© ASHLEIGH BRILLIANT 1988.

Ashleigh Brilliant
SANTA BARBARA

© ASHLEIGH BRILLIANT 1988.   POT-SHOTS NO. 4444.

Ashleigh
Brilliant
SANTA BARBARA

THINK HOW SAD
YOU'LL BE

IF I DIE
BEFORE HEARING
WHAT YOU'VE
ALWAYS
WANTED
TO TELL ME.

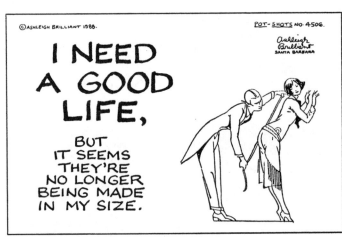

© ASHLEIGH BRILLIANT 1988.   POT-SHOTS NO. 4506.

Ashleigh
Brilliant
SANTA BARBARA

I NEED
A GOOD
LIFE,

BUT
IT SEEMS
THEY'RE
NO LONGER
BEING MADE
IN MY SIZE.

© ASHLEIGH BRILLIANT 1988.   POT-SHOTS NO. 4647.

EVEN IF
WE ONLY
DIE ONCE,

ISN'T THAT
ONCE
TOO OFTEN?

Ashleigh Brilliant
SANTA BARBARA

© ASHLEIGH BRILLIANT 1988.   POT-SHOTS NO. 4461.

WHEN THEY FINALLY ABOLISH DEATH,

IT WILL BE
A BIG WEIGHT OFF MY MIND.

Ashleigh Brilliant
SANTA BARBARA

© ASHLEIGH BRILLIANT 1988.   POT-SHOTS NO. 4744.

I CAN'T ALWAYS CREEP UP ON MY PROBLEMS ~

SOMETIMES
THEY
HEAR ME
COMING,
AND
TAKE COVER.

Ashleigh Brilliant
SANTA BARBARA

© ASHLEIGH BRILLIANT 1988.   *Ashleigh Brilliant* SANTA BARBARA   POT-SHOTS NO. 4508.

IF MY LIFE CAN'T HAVE BOTH COMFORT AND MEANING,

I'D PREFER
MEANINGLESS COMFORT
TO
UNCOMFORTABLE MEANING.

© ASHLEIGH BRILLIANT 1989.   POT-SHOTS NO. 4796.

THE ONLY TIME
I FIND MORE DIFFICULT
THAN
MORNINGS

IS
THE REST
OF
THE DAY.

Ashleigh Brilliant
SANTA BARBARA

© ASHLEIGH BRILLIANT 1988.   POT-SHOTS NO. 4731.

It's easier for me
to make
lifetime
commitments,

when
I realize
how
temporary
they are.

Ashleigh
Brilliant

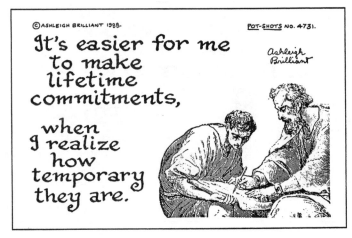

© ASHLEIGH BRILLIANT 1989.   POT-SHOTS NO. 4849

THINGS WERE
MUCH
BETTER,

BEFORE
THEY
MADE
ALL
THE
IMPROVEMENTS.

Ashleigh
Brilliant
SANTA BARBARA

POT-SHOTS NO. 4536.

I CAN
ONLY CONCLUDE
THAT
MY EXISTENCE
CAME ABOUT
AS THE RESULT
OF
SOME KIND OF
MISUNDERSTANDING.

©ASHLEIGH BRILLIANT 1988   Ashleigh Brilliant
SANTA BARBARA

©ASHLEIGH BRILLIANT 1988.   Ashleigh Brilliant SANTA BARBARA   POT-SHOTS NO. 4720

Is life
the kind
of puzzle
you put together,
or the kind
you
take apart?

©ASHLEIGH BRILLIANT 1988.   POT-SHOTS NO. 4715.

LIFE IS CRUEL

— THAT'S WHY
IT'S SO IMPORTANT
FOR PEOPLE
TO BE KIND.

Ashleigh Brilliant
SANTA BARBARA

POT-SHOTS NO. 4453.

THE DAY AFTER I DIE

IS
A DAY
I'LL NEVER
FORGET.

Ashleigh Brilliant
SANTA BARBARA © ASHLEIGH BRILLIANT 1988.

© ASHLEIGH BRILLIANT 1989. POT-SHOTS NO. 4852.

CONGRATULATIONS!

YOU HAVE WON
A LIFETIME
SUPPLY
OF
LIFE.

Ashleigh
Brilliant
SANTA BARBARA

© ASHLEIGH BRILLIANT 1989. POT-SHOTS NO. 4910.

THIS STARTED OUT TO BE A GOOD DAY~

BUT
THEN
I GOT UP.

Ashleigh Brilliant
SANTA BARBARA

© ASHLEIGH BRILLIANT 1989. POT-SHOTS NO. 4830

IT'S FRIGHTENING TO THINK HOW MANY THINGS MAY BE WAITING TO HAPPEN OVER MY DEAD BODY.

Ashleigh Brilliant
SANTA BARBARA

© ASHLEIGH BRILLIANT 1989. POT-SHOTS NO. 4564.

IT'S HARD TO MAKE PROGRESS, WHEN I'VE NO IDEA WHICH DIRECTION IS FORWARD.

Ashleigh Brilliant SANTA BARBARA

© ASHLEIGH BRILLIANT 1988. POT-SHOTS NO. 4693.

ISN'T IT REASONABLE TO BE AFRAID, IN A WORLD WHERE THERE'S STILL NO KNOWN CURE FOR DEATH?

Ashleigh Brilliant
SANTA BARBARA

Life and the Other Thing 99

© ASHLEIGH BRILLIANT 1989.   POT-SHOTS NO. 4804.

I HOPE
THEY DON'T
MAKE ME
LEAVE
THE WORLD,

JUST WHEN
LIFE
STARTS TO GET
INTERESTING.

Ashleigh Brilliant
SANTA BARBARA

© ASHLEIGH BRILLIANT 1989.   POT-SHOTS NO. 4839.

Ashleigh Brilliant
SANTA BARBARA

WE DON'T
STOP
THINKING
ABOUT
PEOPLE
JUST
BECAUSE
THEY'VE DIED,

— BUT THEY MAY
STOP THINKING
ABOUT US.

POT-SHOTS NO. 4969.   © ASHLEIGH BRILLIANT 1989.

I HAVE ALREADY
PAID THE PRICE
OF SUCCESS,

BUT
AM STILL
AWAITING
DELIVERY.

Ashleigh Brilliant
SANTA BARBARA

WHAT COMPENSATION AM I ENTITLED TO

FOR THE WEAR AND TEAR OF DAILY LIFE?

Ashleigh Brilliant
SANTA BARBARA

I CAN HARDLY WAIT UNTIL IMMORTALITY COMES BACK IN STYLE.

Ashleigh Brilliant
SANTA BARBARA

POT-SHOTS NO. 4999

I DIDN'T PAY ANYTHING FOR MY BODY,

BUT THE MAINTENANCE COSTS ARE RATHER HIGH.

Ashleigh Brilliant
SANTA BARBARA

Chapter VIII

Mind Over Mutter

This chapter will do what it can to help you avoid travel sickness on your journey through life, at least by providing some appropriate postcard prescriptions for the health of your Body and Mind.

Once again, however (as with our friends Life and Death), you may need some help in determining which of these two inter-connected pieces of equipment is which — so I hope the following hints may be of some value:

Your Body is the one that gets up in the morning (while your Mind has been busy going places and doing things all night).

Your Mind is the only one you can (normally) change, give somebody else a piece of, keep people in, or (in extreme cases) be driven out of.

Minds are in some ways more secure than Bodies, since only Bodies have to worry about snatchers, and only Bodies require their own guards.

On the other hand, only Minds are subject to being blown, cast back, slipped, or boggled.

Nobody seems to care if you have a one-track Body, or if you Body your own business. But then nobody (no matter how offensive your thinking) is likely to accuse you of having "Mind Odor."

As a final caution, please remember that it is currently considered unfashionable for Bodies to be worn too broad, or Minds too narrow.

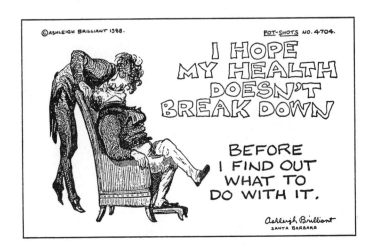

© ASHLEIGH BRILLIANT 1988. POT-SHOTS NO. 4704.

I HOPE MY HEALTH DOESN'T BREAK DOWN

BEFORE I FIND OUT WHAT TO DO WITH IT.

Ashleigh Brilliant
SANTA BARBARA

© ASHLEIGH BRILLIANT 1988. POT-SHOTS NO. 4780.

Ashleigh Brilliant
SANTA BARBARA

WHY DO I SO OFTEN FORGET THE IMPORTANT,

WHILE THE TRIVIAL IS INDELIBLY RECORDED ON MY MEMORY?

© ASHLEIGH BRILLIANT 1988. POT-SHOTS NO. 4623.

WHAT MAKES SOME CRAZY PEOPLE SOUND VERY CONVINCING

IS THAT THEY THEMSELVES BELIEVE EVERYTHING THEY SAY.

Ashleigh Brilliant
SANTA BARBARA

© ASHLEIGH BRILLIANT 1988.   POT-SHOTS NO. 4747.

There's one artist whose work I always carry with me:

my dentist.

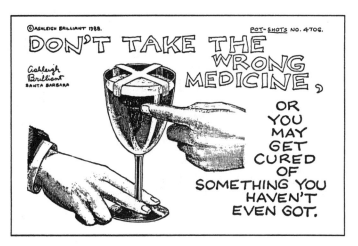

© ASHLEIGH BRILLIANT 1988.   POT-SHOTS NO. 4706.

DON'T TAKE THE WRONG MEDICINE, OR YOU MAY GET CURED OF SOMETHING YOU HAVEN'T EVEN GOT.

© ASHLEIGH BRILLIANT 1988.   POT-SHOTS NO. 4724.

WHY IS HEALING SUCH HARD WORK, WHEN GETTING SICK TAKES SO LITTLE EFFORT?

© ASHLEIGH BRILLIANT 1988.   POT-SHOTS NO. 4524.

You can extend your life in the middle more easily than at the ends.

Ashleigh Brilliant
SANTA BARBARA

© ASHLEIGH BRILLIANT 1988.   POT-SHOTS NO. 4545.

MY FIRST LINE OF DEFENSE AGAINST REALITY

IS CALLED SLEEP.

Ashleigh Brilliant
SANTA BARBARA

© ASHLEIGH BRILLIANT 1988.   POT-SHOTS NO. 4522.

KEEP EATING PERFECTLY NORMALLY,

Ashleigh Brilliant
SANTA BARBARA

AND EVENTUALLY

YOU MAY HAVE A PERFECTLY NORMAL HEART ATTACK.

OF COURSE
I BELIEVE
IT! ~

I SAW IT
IN MY OWN
HALLUCINATION.

IF YOU THINK
YOU'RE
GOING
CRAZY,

YOU'RE
PROBABLY
NOT.

TWO OF
THE GREATEST
TIME MACHINES
EVER
INVENTED

ARE CALLED
MEMORY
AND
IMAGINATION.

POT-SHOTS NO. 4633.

NOT ALL GAMBLERS ARE SMOKERS,

BUT ALL SMOKERS ARE GAMBLERS.

Ashleigh Brilliant SANTA BARBARA

POT-SHOTS NO. 4390.

ALTHOUGH IT'S QUITE NORMAL TO DREAM,

WHAT HAPPENS IN MY DREAMS IS ANYTHING BUT NORMAL.

Ashleigh Brilliant SANTA BARBARA

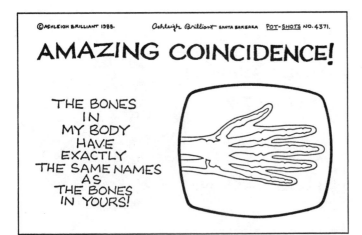

Ashleigh Brilliant SANTA BARBARA POT-SHOTS NO. 4371.

AMAZING COINCIDENCE!

THE BONES IN MY BODY HAVE EXACTLY THE SAME NAMES AS THE BONES IN YOURS!

POT-SHOTS NO. 4443.

PRESERVE
EVERYTHING
THAT MIGHT BE
OF INTEREST TO
FUTURE
GENERATIONS ~

INCLUDING,
IF POSSIBLE,
YOURSELF.

©ASHLEIGH BRILLIANT 1988.

©ASHLEIGH BRILLIANT 1985.

POT-SHOTS NO. 3540.

Ashleigh Brilliant
SANTA BARBARA

NO MATTER
HOW MUCH
I EXERCISE
MY BODY,

IT REFUSES
TO GO AWAY,
AND LEAVE
ME ALONE.

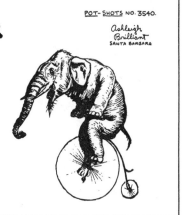

©ASHLEIGH BRILLIANT 1988.

POT-SHOTS NO. 4438.

IF YOU ALWAYS TRY
TO BE
LOGICAL,

YOU
PROBABLY
WON'T EVER HAVE
MUCH SORROW,

OR
MUCH FUN.

Ashleigh Brilliant
SANTA BARBARA

© ASHLEIGH BRILLIANT 1989.   POT-SHOTS NO. 4880.

FOR SOME REASON,

IT'S HARD
TO BE
QUITE AS
DEPRESSED
WHILE
EXERCISING,
AS WHILE
SITTING STILL.

Ashleigh Brilliant
SANTA BARBARA

© ASHLEIGH BRILLIANT 1989.   POT-SHOTS NO 4957.

DESPITE ALL ATTEMPTS,

NO
LIVING PERSON
HAS YET
BEEN ABLE
TO FORGET

FASTER
THAN A
COMPUTER.

Ashleigh Brilliant
SANTA BARBARA

POT-SHOTS NO. 4591.

CAN A BRUISED EGO

BE
CONSIDERED
A WORK-RELATED
INJURY?

© ASHLEIGH BRILLIANT 1988

Ashleigh Brilliant
SANTA BARBARA

MY DREAMS KEEP BEING INTERRUPTED BY COMMERCIAL MESSAGES.

© ASHLEIGH BRILLIANT 1988.   POT-SHOTS NO. 4521.

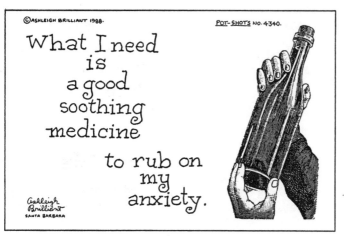

What I need is a good soothing medicine to rub on my anxiety.

© ASHLEIGH BRILLIANT 1988.   POT-SHOTS NO. 4340.

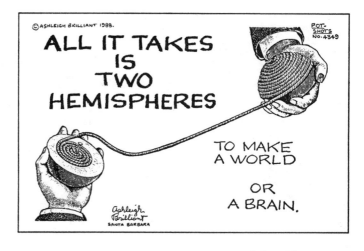

ALL IT TAKES IS TWO HEMISPHERES TO MAKE A WORLD OR A BRAIN.

© ASHLEIGH BRILLIANT 1988.   POT-SHOTS NO. 4349.

© ASHLEIGH BRILLIANT 1989.   POT-SHOTS NO. 4971.

THERE IS A SADNESS IN MY HEAD,

WHICH COULD BE FATAL IF IT SPREADS TO MY HEART.

Ashleigh Brilliant
SANTA BARBARA

© ASHLEIGH BRILLIANT 1989.   POT-SHOTS NO. 4842.

IT TAKES VERY LITTLE DIGGING

TO PLANT DOUBTS IN MY MIND.

Ashleigh Brilliant
SANTA BARBARA

© ASHLEIGH BRILLIANT 1988.   POT-SHOTS NO. 4515.

MY MEMORY WOULD BE EASIER TO CONSULT,

IF IT HAD A GOOD INDEX.

Ashleigh Brilliant
SANTA BARBARA

© ASHLEIGH BRILLIANT 1988.

POT-SHOTS NO. 4331.

IF THIS IS INSANITY,

WHY DID I STAY SANE SO LONG?

Ashleigh Brilliant
SANTA BARBARA

POT-SHOTS NO. 4379.

I CAN'T IMAGINE THE UNIVERSE BEGINNING OR ENDING ~

IF I COULD, I'D BE AFRAID OF MY IMAGINATION.

Ashleigh Brilliant
SANTA BARBARA

© ASHLEIGH BRILLIANT 1988.

Pot-Shots  BY ASHLEIGH BRILLIANT

© ASHLEIGH BRILLIANT 1988.

POT-SHOTS NO. 4374.

ANYTHING CAN HAPPEN TO ME TOMORROW,

BUT AT LEAST NOTHING MORE CAN HAPPEN TO ME YESTERDAY.

Ashleigh Brilliant
SANTA BARBARA

Chapter IX

Time Pieces

At this point on the itinerary, we pause to admire the work of that famous performer, Time, whose acts always get top billing in Nature's variety show, combining, as they do, not only comedy and drama, but also dance, and a bit of magic. The finesse of these productions is all the more remarkable when you consider the paranoia with which Time must face the perpetual risk of being marked, beaten, killed, or (no doubt a fate even worse) just frittered away.

Time, however, is also a skilled contortionist and escape artist, having the ability to stretch and contract, and, by means of a simple device called a "nick," can achieve amazingly suspenseful effects.

Somewhat camera-shy, for obvious reasons, Time is also apparently a master of disguises. Certain special observers called poets have tried to render an image, but their depictions vary astonishingly. Some claim to have seen something like a bird on the wing, an ever-rolling stream, a cradle endlessly rocking, or a finger writing on the wall. Others thought they saw a vagrant gipsy, a weaver, or somebody on the march. There are even those (among the more affluent poets) to whom Time looked very much like money.

Whatever your own perception, I hope the following messages will persuade you that Time is on your side (as well as on your front and back, and all the way down through your middle).

POT-SHOTS NO. 4389.

THE FUTURE SEEMS TO BE IN GOOD HANDS ~

IT'S THE PAST I'M WORRIED ABOUT.

©ASHLEIGH BRILLIANT 1988.

Ashleigh Brilliant
SANTA BARBARA

POT-SHOTS NO 4970.

©ASHLEIGH BRILLIANT 1989.

HISTORY WOULD HAVE BEEN VERY DIFFERENT, IF VICTORY ALWAYS WENT TO THE SIDE WITH THE BEST SONGS.

Ashleigh Brilliant
SANTA BARBARA

POT-SHOTS NO. 4843.

©ASHLEIGH BRILLIANT 1989.

LIVE LONG ENOUGH, AND YOU MAY FIND YOUR ENTIRE LIFE IN A MUSEUM.

Ashleigh Brilliant
SANTA BARBARA

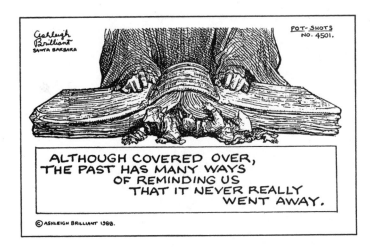

ALGHLEIGH BRILLIANT SANTA BARBARA

POT-SHOTS NO. 4501.

ALTHOUGH COVERED OVER,
THE PAST HAS MANY WAYS
OF REMINDING US
THAT IT NEVER REALLY
WENT AWAY.

© ASHLEIGH BRILLIANT 1988.

© ASHLEIGH BRILLIANT 1988.

POT-SHOTS NO. 4383.

I CAN'T
STOP
THE
WORLD
CHANGING

BUT
THAT'S FAIR,
BECAUSE
THE WORLD
CAN'T STOP
ME CHANGING
EITHER.

Ashleigh Brilliant
SANTA BARBARA

© ASHLEIGH BRILLIANT 1989.

POT-SHOTS NO. 4932.

THERE'S NO
GOING BACK~

ALL THE
SPACE
BEHIND US
IS NOW
OCCUPIED
BY SOMETHING
CALLED
THE PAST.

Ashleigh Brilliant SANTA BARBARA

©ASHLEIGH BRILLIANT 1988.   POT-SHOTS NO. 4402.

How did I reach
the other side
of so many things
that were once
in the future?

Ashleigh
Brilliant
SANTA BARBARA

POT-SHOTS NO. 4404.

I DON'T
NEED TO BE
REMINDED
THAT
TIME
IS
PASSING~

I NEED
HELP
IN
FOR-
GET-
TING
IT.

©ASHLEIGH BRILLIANT

Ashleigh
Brilliant
SANTA BARBARA

©ASHLEIGH BRILLIANT 1989.   POT-SHOTS NO. 4799.

I'M IN NO HURRY ~

PLEASE TELL GOD
TO TAKE HIS TIME
DISPOSING
OF
MY
CASE.

Ashleigh
Brilliant
SANTA BARBARA

POT-SHOTS NO. 3876.

IF YOU CAN IMAGINE THE FUTURE,

YOU'RE HALF-WAY THERE.

©ASHLEIGH BRILLIANT 1985.

Ashleigh Brilliant
SANTA BARBARA

©ASHLEIGH BRILLIANT 1989.

POT-SHOTS NO. 4795

I HAVE TO HURRY,

BECAUSE THERE'S A DEADLINE CALLED THE END OF MY LIFE.

Ashleigh Brilliant
SANTA BARBARA

POT-SHOTS NO. 4364.

THE PUNISHMENT FOR LAUGHING AT PEOPLE IN THE PAST

IS THAT EVENTUALLY YOU BECOME ONE OF THEM.

©ASHLEIGH BRILLIANT 1988.

Ashleigh Brilliant
SANTA BARBARA

© ASHLEIGH BRILLIANT 1988. POT-SHOTS NO. 4470.

WHAT MAKES IT SO HARD
TO LEARN FROM HISTORY
IS THAT HISTORY ISN'T OVER YET.

© ASHLEIGH BRILLIANT 1988. POT-SHOTS NO. 4553.

IT'S OBVIOUS
WHAT MY FUTURE
CONSISTS OF:

A LITTLE TIME,
FOLLOWED BY
A LOT OF
INFINITY.

Ashleigh Brilliant
SANTA BARBARA

POT-SHOTS NO. 4460.

NOBODY SHOULD
GET OLD
WITHOUT GOOD REASON,
AND I'VE NEVER YET
HEARD A GOOD REASON.

© ASHLEIGH BRILLIANT 1988.

Ashleigh Brilliant
SANTA BARBARA

© ASHLEIGH BRILLIANT 1989.   POT-SHOTS NO. 4813.

MY HOPE
IS
TO GET
ALL THE WAY
THROUGH LIFE
WITHOUT
HAVING IT
COST ME
ANYTHING.

Ashleigh Brilliant
SANTA BARBARA

© ASHLEIGH BRILLIANT 1989.   POT-SHOTS NO. 4871.

As far
as
we
know

this
is
only
half-
way

through
eter-
nity.

Ashleigh
Brilliant
SANTA BARBARA

© ASHLEIGH BRILLIANT 1989   POT-SHOTS NO. 4814.

THERE ARE
1440
MINUTES
IN A DAY,

BUT
ONE BAD ONE
CAN SPOIL
ALL THE REST.

Ashleigh
Brilliant
SANTA BARBARA

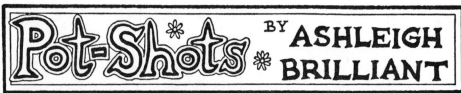

©ASHLEIGH BRILLIANT 1988.

POT-SHOTS NO. 4642.

WHAT GOOD
IS IT
TO HAVE
THE KEY
TO WISDOM,

IF I CAN'T
FIND
THE LOCK?

Ashleigh Brilliant
SANTA BARBARA

Chapter X

Lost and Profound

By now it must surely be time for refreshment, so I offer your heart and soul (both no doubt equally famished) some morsels of Religion and Philosophy from my portable pantry of profundities.

In case you doubt my qualifications to address these topics, please be advised that, in addition to many years of penal servitude in public school, I served a concurrent sentence, from age 8 to 13, in a school of Religion conducted in a Washington, D.C. Synagogue; and that the University of California at Berkeley has officially declared me to be a Doctor of Philosophy [See documents, page 13.]. I must admit that I learned very little of value in either place — and absolutely nothing about Religion or Philosophy — but of course, that has nothing at all to do with being qualified.

The public at large is probably not aware of the fact that we professional deep thinkers are, as a group, very much concerned about maintaining high ethical standards. Currently at issue is the problem of whether we have the right to go out on strike — and whether anybody would notice if we did. Then there are the vexed questions of how discarded thoughts can be safely disposed of, and whether we should demand separate areas in public places for deep-thinkers, shallow-thinkers, and non-thinkers. Still also unresolved is the long-standing debate over whether it is ethical to think about other people without their consent.

Obviously, the discussions might get pretty heated if we ever held a convention, but, for better or worse, such a gathering is hardly feasible, since, before they can do anything on the surface, deep thinkers always require many days of decompression.

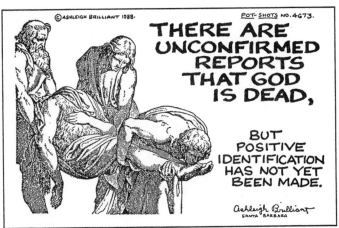

© ASHLEIGH BRILLIANT 1988. POT-SHOTS NO. 4673.

THERE ARE UNCONFIRMED REPORTS THAT GOD IS DEAD,

BUT POSITIVE IDENTIFICATION HAS NOT YET BEEN MADE.

Ashleigh Brilliant
SANTA BARBARA

© ASHLEIGH BRILLIANT 1989. POT-SHOTS NO. 4543.

I CAN'T EAT THIS FOOD ~

IT CAME OUT OF THE GROUND!

Ashleigh Brilliant
SANTA BARBARA

© ASHLEIGH BRILLIANT 1989. POT-SHOTS NO. 4936.

A LITTLE PRAYER

GOES A LONG WAY.

Ashleigh Brilliant
SANTA BARBARA

© ASHLEIGH BRILLIANT 1989.   POT-SHOTS NO. 4801.

LET'S TAKE THE ROAD TO HELL~

IT HAS MUCH BETTER PAVING.

Ashleigh Brilliant
SANTA BARBARA

© ASHLEIGH BRILLIANT 1988.   POT-SHOTS NO. 4687.

Ashleigh Brilliant
SANTA BARBARA

This may be the only world we'll ever know ~

that's the beauty and the tragedy of it.

POT-SHOTS NO. 4585.   © ASHLEIGH BRILLIANT 1988.

GOD SEEMS TO CONSIDER MY CASE HOPELESS,

BUT I WOULD LIKE TO HAVE A SECOND OPINION.

Ashleigh Brilliant
SANTA BARBARA

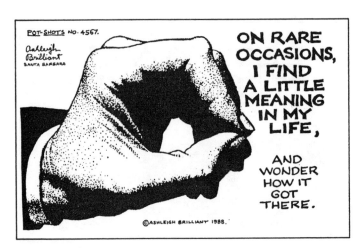

POT-SHOTS NO. 4567.

Ashleigh Brilliant
SANTA BARBARA

ON RARE OCCASIONS, I FIND A LITTLE MEANING IN MY LIFE, AND WONDER HOW IT GOT THERE.

©ASHLEIGH BRILLIANT 1988.

©ASHLEIGH BRILLIANT 1989.

POT-SHOTS NO. 4819.

I WOULD NOT HAVE THOUGHT THIS WORLD POSSIBLE, IF I HADN'T BEEN BROUGHT HERE TO WITNESS IT.

Ashleigh Brilliant
SANTA BARBARA

©ASHLEIGH BRILLIANT 1988.

POT-SHOTS NO. 4566.

Ashleigh Brilliant
SANTA BARBARA

I'M AFRAID THERE MAY BE TWO GODS, AND EACH THINKS THE OTHER IS TAKING CARE OF ME.

It's strange that the identity of God is still a mystery, since he's left so many clues.

THE MORE PEOPLE THERE ARE WHO SIMPLY CANNOT COPE WITH REALITY, THE LESS ALONE I FEEL.

HOW CAN I BE SURE THIS IS THE REAL WORLD, AND NOT JUST A VERY CLEVER IMITATION?

© ASHLEIGH BRILLIANT 1989

POT-SHOTS NO. 4931.

EVEN
A
MEANINGLESS
LIFE

MAY
CONTAIN
MANY
GOOD
BREAKFASTS.

Ashleigh Brilliant
SANTA BARBARA

© ASHLEIGH BRILLIANT 1988.

POT-SHOTS NO. 4356.

EVEN IN HELL,

Ashleigh
Brilliant
SANTA BARBARA

SOME DAYS
ARE WORSE
THAN
OTHERS:

IT'S
THE
UNCERTAINTY
THAT
MAKES
IT SO
HELLISH.

© ASHLEIGH BRILLIANT 1988.

POT-SHOTS NO. 4375.

AM I
A
DISAPPOINTMENT
TO GOD,

OR
WAS HE
NEVER REALLY
EXPECTING MUCH
FROM ME?

Ashleigh Brilliant
SANTA BARBARA

© ASHLEIGH BRILLIANT 1989.

POT-SHOTS NO. 4844.

IF YOU DON'T KNOW WHAT THE TRUTH IS,

HOW CAN YOU EVER TELL A LIE?

Ashleigh Brilliant
SANTA BARBARA

POT-SHOTS NO. 4352.

GOD EXCELS AT CONSTRUCTION AND DEMOLITION,

BUT DOES NOT SEEM TO WORK ACCORDING TO ANY FIXED SCHEDULE.

Ashleigh Brilliant
SANTA BARBARA

© ASHLEIGH BRILLIANT 1988.

© ASHLEIGH BRILLIANT 1989.

POT-SHOTS NO. 4825.

GIVE US THIS DAY

OUR DAILY DAY.

Ashleigh Brilliant
SANTA BARBARA

© ASHLEIGH BRILLIANT 1989. POT-SHOTS NO. 4823.

𝒥he next best thing
to experiencing
heaven

is
believing
in it.

Ashleigh Brilliant
SANTA BARBARA

© ASHLEIGH BRILLIANT 1989. POT-SHOTS NO. 4821.

NO MATTER HOW OFTEN I TALK TO GOD,

HE NEVER TELLS ME ANYTHING I DON'T ALREADY KNOW.

Ashleigh Brilliant
SANTA BARBARA

© ASHLEIGH BRILLIANT 1988. POT-SHOTS NO. 4631.

PLEASE DON'T ENLIGHTEN ME ~

LIFE IS HARD ENOUGH
WITHOUT KNOWING
WHO I AM
AND
WHERE
I'M
GOING.

Ashleigh Brilliant
SANTA BARBARA

© ASHLEIGH BRILLIANT 1988.   POT-SHOTS NO. 4480.

I HAVE NO SPECIAL MISSION HERE ON EARTH ~

OR,
IF I HAVE,
MY ORDERS
HAVEN'T YET
ARRIVED.

© ASHLEIGH BRILLIANT 1989.   POT-SHOTS NO. 4913.

I HOPE
YOU FIND

AS MUCH
CONSOLATION

IN YOUR FAITH

AS I FIND
IN MY
SKEPTICISM.

POT-SHOTS NO. 4805. © ASHLEIGH BRILLIANT 1989.

IT'S EASIER
BELIEVING
EVERYTHING
HAPPENS
FOR THE
BEST,

IF WE
LEAVE OUT
MY BEST
AND
YOUR BEST.

POT-SHOTS NO. 4516. Ashleigh Brilliant SANTA BARBARA

The size of your mind's opening determines how much light comes through to illuminate your soul.

©ASHLEIGH BRILLIANT 1988.

©ASHLEIGH BRILLIANT 1988. POT-SHOTS NO. 4556.

You don't have to be religious to believe that more exists than we can ever know about.

Ashleigh Brilliant
SANTA BARBARA

©ASHLEIGH BRILLIANT 1988. POT-SHOTS NO. 4542.

Ashleigh Brilliant
SANTA BARBARA

THE MOST CONVENIENT TIME TO BE FORGIVEN FOR MY SINS

IS BEFORE I COMMIT THEM.

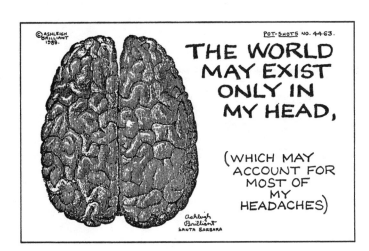

© ASHLEIGH BRILLIANT 1988.

POT-SHOTS NO. 4463.

THE WORLD MAY EXIST ONLY IN MY HEAD,

(WHICH MAY ACCOUNT FOR MOST OF MY HEADACHES)

Ashleigh Brilliant
SANTA BARBARA

© ASHLEIGH BRILLIANT 1988.

POT-SHOTS NO. 4740.

THE GOD WHO INVENTED LAUGHTER

CAN'T BE ALL BAD.

Ashleigh Brilliant
SANTA BARBARA

Pot-Shots BY ASHLEIGH BRILLIANT

POT-SHOTS NO. 4983.

IF YOU START
BY BELIEVING
IN LITTLE
IMPOSSIBILITIES,

YOU CAN
TRAIN YOURSELF
TO BELIEVE
IN BIG ONES.

Ashleigh Brilliant
SANTA BARBARA

Chapter XI

Another Think Coming

Possibly the greatest thinker of all time was the anonymous genius who invented the category called "Miscellaneous." Until that inspired moment, large numbers of unclassified thoughts had for countless eons been floating forlornly about the universe, belonging nowhere. Since then, however, they have always had a home — and their home in this book is the present chapter, where they wait eagerly to welcome our specially-arranged visit.

As visitors (just arrived on the Train of Thought), it of course behooves us to remember our manners when meeting a formerly homeless expression, and not to ask it embarrassing questions about delicate matters such as parentage. But, to set your mind at rest, I myself am happy to assert my own paternity in all cases, as attested by the sacrament of Copyright registration. It should in any event be quite apparent that all thoughts residing here are now perfectly respectable, and any resentful tone you may detect in some of them can surely be excused in view of their earlier hardships.

So, before entering, please wipe your feet of all prejudice, and have your handkerchief ready, since many of these musings are quite sensitive, and certainly none are to be sneezed at. I'm sure you wouldn't want to be responsible for accidentally extinguishing one of my brain-children, would you? — Perish the thought!

POT-SHOTS NO. 4575.

THE ONLY WAY OUT OF SOME TROUBLES

IS NEVER TO GET INTO THEM.

© ASHLEIGH BRILLIANT 1988.

Ashleigh Brilliant
SANTA BARBARA

© ASHLEIGH BRILLIANT 1988.

POT-SHOTS NO. 4574.

THE DIFFERENCE BETWEEN SCIENCE AND MAGIC

IS THAT MAGICIANS USUALLY KNOW WHAT THEY'RE DOING.

Ashleigh Brilliant
SANTA BARBARA

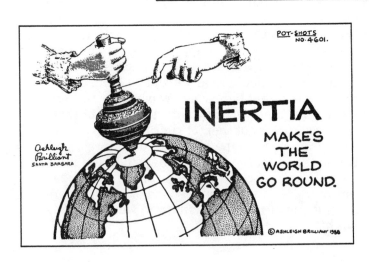

POT-SHOTS NO. 4601.

INERTIA

MAKES THE WORLD GO ROUND.

Ashleigh Brilliant
SANTA BARBARA

© ASHLEIGH BRILLIANT 1988

© ASHLEIGH BRILLIANT 1988.

POT-SHOTS NO. 4485.

IF WE COULD KNOW IN ADVANCE WHETHER OR NOT EXPLORATION WOULD BE VALUABLE,

IT WOULDN'T BE EXPLORATION.

Ashleigh Brilliant
SANTA BARBARA

POT-SHOTS NO. 4396.

Ashleigh Brilliant
SANTA BARBARA

WHY IS IT SO MUCH HARDER

TO MAINTAIN A WINNING STREAK

THAN TO MAINTAIN A LOSING STREAK?

© ASHLEIGH BRILLIANT 1988.

POT-SHOTS NO. 4750.

GREATEST OF ALL HUMAN RIGHTS:

FREEDOM TO GRUMBLE.

© ASHLEIGH BRILLIANT 1988.

Ashleigh Brilliant
SANTA BARBARA

© ASHLEIGH BRILLIANT 1988.   POT-SHOTS NO. 4751.

I HAVE NOTHING TO HIDE ~

WHICH
MAY BE
WHY
LIFE SEEMS
SO DULL.

Ashleigh Brilliant SANTA BARBARA

© ASHLEIGH BRILLIANT 1988.   POT-SHOTS NO. 4770.

Ashleigh
Brilliant
SANTA BARBARA

Perhaps it's best
to keep
some dreams
in my heart,

where they'll
always be
safe from
disappointment.

POT-SHOTS NO. 4715.

AS A GENERAL RULE,

IT'S BEST
TO PUT
ONLY ONE
FOOT
FORWARD
AT A TIME.

© ASHLEIGH BRILLIANT 1988.

Ashleigh Brilliant
SANTA BARBARA

© ASHLEIGH BRILLIANT 1988. POT-SHOTS NO. 4544.

THE BEST KIND OF CAPTIVITY

IS
THE KIND
YOU CAN
ESCAPE FROM
AND
RETURN TO
AT WILL.

Ashleigh Brilliant
SANTA BARBARA

© ASHLEIGH BRILLIANT 1989. POT-SHOTS NO. 4789

STATISTICALLY, THE ODDS AGAINST REALITY ARE OVERWHELMING ~

~ WHAT DOES THIS SAY ABOUT STATISTICS?

Ashleigh Brilliant
SANTA BARBARA

© ASHLEIGH BRILLIANT 1989. POT-SHOTS NO. 4883.

BEING FAMOUS

MEANS
BEING
CLOSER TO
MANY
PEOPLE
THAN MOST
OF THEM
CAN EVER BE
TO YOU.

Ashleigh Brilliant
SANTA BARBARA

POT-SHOTS NO. 4920. ©ASHLEIGH BRILLIANT 1989

I'VE BEEN
SENTENCED
TO LIFE
ON EARTH,

WITHOUT
EVER
BEING TOLD
THE CHARGE.

Ashleigh Brilliant
SANTA BARBARA

©ASHLEIGH BRILLIANT 1989.

POT-SHOTS
NO. 4912.

THE SAFEST
PLAN IS
NEVER
TO DO
ANYTHING
FOR THE
FIRST
TIME.

Ashleigh Brilliant
SANTA BARBARA

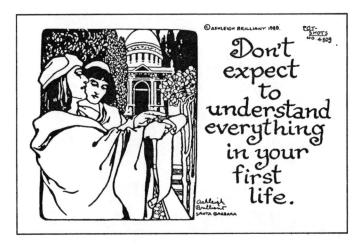

©ASHLEIGH BRILLIANT 1989.

POT-SHOTS
NO. 4809.

Don't
expect
to
understand
everything
in your
first
life.

Ashleigh Brilliant
SANTA BARBARA

THE BEST THING ABOUT NEVER HAVING A HOME

IS THAT YOU CAN NEVER BE AN EXILE.

HOW LONG MUST WE WAIT PATIENTLY

FOR WHAT WILL PROBABLY NEVER HAPPEN

UNTIL WE STOP WAITING PATIENTLY?

MANKIND IS A NUMEROUS SPECIES,

BUT PEOPLE WILL NEVER AGAIN OUTNUMBER MACHINES.

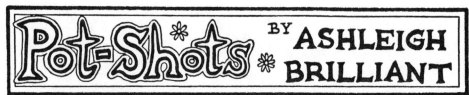

POT-SHOTS NO. 4464.

BEHIND
THE BIG
QUESTIONS
LIKE:
WHAT IS LIFE?

ARE OTHER
IMPORTANT QUESTIONS
LIKE:
WHAT IS
FOR DINNER?

Ashleigh Brilliant
SANTA BARBARA

Chapter XII

Light at the End

Those who claim to be in the know often tell the rest of us that the ending of life is like emerging from some sort of tunnel into an overpoweringly bright light. Assuming that this is true, and that it really *is* lighter "out there," all I can do in the meantime is try to lighten things up at least a little "in here," where we are, especially in this concluding chapter. After all, traveling through our current existence can sometimes be a heavy experience, and, considering how much we have been through together on this trip, I feel I owe you some lighter thoughts to help you float up out of this book and away to wherever you are going next.

So prepare to shed the ballast of mental gravity, and alert your brain to take aboard a fresh supply of less weighty (but equally Brilliant) enlightenments, all wrapped in my most buoyant good wishes.

Before alighting, please check to make sure you have not left anything but a good impression in any of the previous chapters. I have (for the most part) enjoyed being your guide, and hope you will recommend my cerebral services to your friends. As you leave, please watch your step, mind your head, and (if possible) head your mind in some happy new direction.

© ASHLEIGH BRILLIANT 1988.

POT-SHOTS NO. 4779.

Ashleigh Brilliant SANTA BARBARA

FOR PERMANENT HAPPINESS

FIND A MOMENT IN WHICH ALL IS WELL, AND REFUSE TO LEAVE IT.

© ASHLEIGH BRILLIANT 1988.

POT-SHOTS NO. 4578.

IF WE MUST HAVE EVOLUTION,

WHY COULDN'T IT BE BASED ON THE SURVIVAL OF THE SWEETEST?

Ashleigh Brilliant SANTA BARBARA

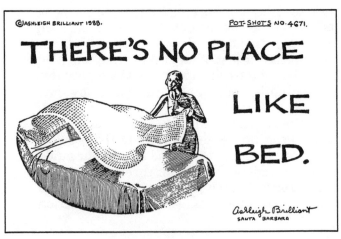

© ASHLEIGH BRILLIANT 1988.

POT-SHOTS NO. 4671.

THERE'S NO PLACE LIKE BED.

Ashleigh Brilliant SANTA BARBARA

© ASHLEIGH BRILLIANT 1988.   *Ashleigh Brilliant* SANTA BARBARA   POT-SHOTS NO. 4664.

I'D GLADLY
PARTICIPATE
IN ANY
EXPERIMENT
TO TEST
THE
EFFECTS
ON ME OF
SUDDEN
GREAT
WEALTH.

© ASHLEIGH BRILLIANT 1988.   POT-SHOTS NO. 4717.

IF IT ISN'T GOOD FOR
ANYTHING
ELSE,

YOU CAN
ALWAYS
CALL IT
ART.

Ashleigh Brilliant
SANTA BARBARA

© ASHLEIGH BRILLIANT 1988.   POT-SHOTS NO. 4552.

GREAT
SCIENTIFIC
DISCOVERY:

MOST THINGS
IN THE UNIVERSE
ARE TOO BIG
OR TOO SMALL
TO WORRY ABOUT.

Ashleigh Brilliant
SANTA BARBARA

POT-SHOTS NO. 4719.

WHAT COULD POSSIBLY MATTER MORE IN LIFE

THAN A CHEAP MOMENTARY THRILL?

Ashleigh Brilliant SANTA BARBARA

© ASHLEIGH BRILLIANT 1988.

© ASHLEIGH BRILLIANT 1989.

POT-SHOTS NO. 4956.

IN SHEER SELF-DEFENSE,

I HAVE BEEN FORCED TO BECOME A MORE PLEASANT PERSON.

Ashleigh Brilliant SANTA BARBARA

POT-SHOTS NO. 4959

WHAT I NEED

IS SOMETHING TO TAKE MY MIND OFF

FANTASY, ENTERTAINMENT, AND ESCAPE.

© ASHLEIGH BRILLIANT 1989.

Ashleigh Brilliant SANTA BARBARA

POT-SHOTS NO. 4614.

BEAUTY IS ONLY SKIN DEEP

BUT FORTUNATELY, I HAVE VERY DEEP SKIN.

© ASHLEIGH BRILLIANT 1988.

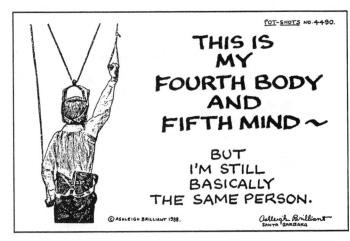

POT-SHOTS NO. 4490.

THIS IS MY FOURTH BODY AND FIFTH MIND ~

BUT I'M STILL BASICALLY THE SAME PERSON.

© ASHLEIGH BRILLIANT 1988.

© ASHLEIGH BRILLIANT 1987.

POT-SHOTS NO. 4061.

WHY CAN'T IT EVER BE DOWNHILL ALL THE WAY THERE AND BACK?

POT-SHOTS NO. 4471.

THE
ROLE
I ALWAYS
PLAY BEST
IS
THAT OF
A VERY
BAD
ACTOR.

©ASHLEIGH BRILLIANT 1988.

Ashleigh Brilliant

©ASHLEIGH BRILLIANT 1988.   POT-SHOTS NO. 4477.

GOOD NEWS
IS COMING IN
FROM
OUTER
SPACE:

THE
GOOD
NEWS
IS
NO NEWS.

Ashleigh Brilliant
SANTA BARBARA

©ASHLEIGH BRILLIANT 1987.   Ashleigh Brilliant SANTA BARBARA   POT-SHOTS NO. 4050.

CAN YOUR
HUSBAND
COME OUT
TO PLAY?

THERE'S NO WAY OF KNOWING WHAT TOO FAR IS, IF NOBODY EVER GOES THERE.

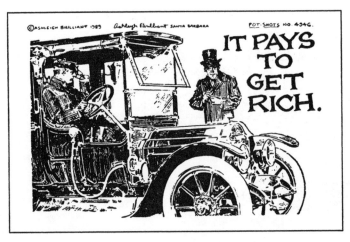

IT PAYS TO GET RICH.

WHY DO I WANT TO CLIMB THAT IMAGINARY MOUNTAIN? — BECAUSE IT ISN'T THERE.

© ASHLEIGH BRILLIANT 1988.   *Ashleigh Brilliant* SANTA BARBARA   POT-SHOTS NO. 4377.

I'M GLAD
I CAN'T
SEE
A THOUSAND
YEARS
INTO
THE FUTURE,

BECAUSE
I LIKE
SURPRISES.

© ASHLEIGH BRILLIANT 1988.   POT-SHOTS NO. 4627.

I KEEP HAVING
A STRANGE,
UNEASY
PREMONITION

THAT
EVERYTHING
IS
GOING TO BE
ALL RIGHT.

Ashleigh Brilliant
SANTA BARBARA

POT-SHOTS NO. 4548.   © ASHLEIGH BRILLIANT 1988.

I CAN
ONLY DO
ONE THING
AT A TIME,

BUT
I CAN
AVOID DOING
MANY THINGS
SIMULTANEOUSLY.

Ashleigh Brilliant
SANTA BARBARA

© ASHLEIGH BRILLIANT 1988.   POT-SHOTS NO. 4732

WHEN I THINK OF SEEKING PLEASURE,

WHY
DO I
SO OFTEN
THINK OF
SEEKING YOU?

Ashleigh Brilliant
SANTA BARBARA

POT-SHOTS NO. 4456.

NOTHING BRIGHTER THAN THE SUN

SHOULD EVER
BE PERMITTED
IN THE SKY.

© ASHLEIGH BRILLIANT 1988.

Ashleigh Brilliant
SANTA BARBARA

© ASHLEIGH BRILLIANT 1988.   POT-SHOTS NO. 4436.

AN OCCASIONAL SMILE

IS
ONE WAY
OF
PREVENTING
ICE
FROM FORMING
ON YOUR FACE.

Ashleigh Brilliant
SANTA BARBARA

Copy Catch

One result of my creation of a totally new form of expression has been the appearance of a flock of imitators. When their imitations begin to look less like a form of flattery and more like actual copies of specific POT-SHOTS® the inevitable result is yet another file for my bulging cabinet of copyright cases.

Often the matter is settled very simply once the problem is pointed out. The infringer apologizes, promises to stop the copying (usually claiming that it was entirely unintentional), and agrees to pay a certain amount of compensation.

But sometimes there is lengthy correspondence between our respective lawyers. The infringers may mistakenly protest that expressions as short as mine cannot be copyrighted! Or in some cases they may speciously argue that they are not really copying, since their words are not exactly the same as mine, or that they have copied only the words and not the picture. Eventually, however, they are always convinced, either in or out of court, that my work can be and is protected by the copyright laws, and that copying can still be copying, even if it is not necessarily word-for-word and even if only the words are involved. In the end there is usually a financial settlement much larger than it would have been without all the fuss.

My purpose in telling you all this is not only to warn off potential infringers (which of course I hope it will do), but also to share with you what has been (for better or worse) a major preoccupation of my unusual career. Just to give you an inkling of the kinds of cases that come up, here are a few actual examples:

1977-79: A Northern California distributor begins selling six "motto" cards which closely resemble POT-SHOTS® each with some slight change in the wording. E.g., where POT-SHOT #445 says, PLEASE RECONSIDER — IT'S SO HARD TO TAKE 'GO TO HELL' FOR AN ANSWER, in his version "PLEASE" is changed to "KINDLY." The man proves to be extremely uncooperative. It actually requires the help of the FBI and a personal stake-out of his headquarters by the infringee (and wife) to gather all necessary evidence. Finally there is a court case which results in a Consent Judgment and Permanent Injunction, and damages of $5,000.

1977-79: A Southern California company producing T-Shirt transfers is found to be copying three POT-SHOTS® including my most famous message (and title of my first book), I MAY NOT BE TOTALLY PERFECT, BUT PARTS OF ME ARE EXCELLENT (#433). Ignoring repeated requests to stop, they are finally taken to court, where a Federal Judge rules that my copyrights are "valid, subsisting, and enforceable," and makes the company pay $18,000 damages and costs.

1981-82: A major American sports magazine publishes, without credit or permission, a photograph of a tennis star displaying the same "PARTS OF ME" message on a T-Shirt. Result: eventual payment of a $2,500 "license fee" and publication of a letter from me in the magazine setting the record straight.

1985-86: A well-known Los Angeles publisher of humor books brings out a collection of so-called "photocopier humor" of the type of messages, supposedly in the public domain, which are freely copied and put up on office bulletin boards. One of them happens to be my POT-SHOT #2576, "IF YOU DON'T KNOW WHERE TO FIND ME, JUST LISTEN FOR THE SOUNDS OF BATTLE." Result: an out-of-court settlement for $1,100.

1983-86: A large San Diego manufacturer of bumper-strips and novelty-pins copies six of my messages, some with altered wording. E.g., instead of "I FEEL MUCH BETTER, NOW THAT I'VE GIVEN UP HOPE" (#519), they have "SINCE I GAVE UP HOPE, I FEEL MUCH BETTER". Result: another court case, another

Consent Judgment and Permanent Injunction, and a "compensation" payment of $7,400.

1986-87: A large Pennsylvania mail-order firm offers in its catalogue uncredited underpants imprinted with, "I MAY NOT BE PERFECT, BUT PARTS OF ME ARE EXCELLENT." (Note absence of "TOTALLY.") My indignation is finally assuaged with a promise to "cease and desist," and a settlement check for $1,000.

1988: A Minneapolis company markets an audio "meditation tape" on which POT-SHOT #586, "EVERY TIME I CLOSE THE DOOR ON REALITY, IT COMES IN THROUGH THE WINDOW," is quoted without permission. In this case, their attitude is quite cooperative, and a settlement agreement for $800 is soon reached.

1987-88: A gigantic U.S. corporation based in Minnesota is caught using my POT-SHOT #212, "ALL I WANT IS A LITTLE MORE THAN I'LL EVER GET," with no permission or acknowledgement, on one of its popular pads of stick-on notes. Eventually I receive both a promise of future royalties and a "license fee" of $6,000.

There are, of course, many other people using POT-SHOTS® material perfectly legitimately in a variety of ways. This naturally involves contacting me first to obtain permission — which, if you have any such usage in mind, I strongly encourage you to do.

[1]They may cite a regulation of the U.S. Copyright Office which says that "short phrases such as names, titles and slogans" are not subject to copyright, but my writings have been ruled in U.S. Federal Court to be *epigrams*, entitled by their originality to full copyright protection. See Richard W. Stim, "Copyright Protection for Literary Phrases," in *New Matter* (Official Publication of the State Bar of California Intellectual Property Section), Vol. 14., No. 4, Winter 1989, pp. 7-12.]

Fan Mail
and Pan Mail

Letters of Credit

Most of the comments I receive from readers are almost embarrassingly complimentary, but many of them also reveal so much about the senders themselves, how they relate to my work, and how it has affected their own lives, that, with an effort, I have decided to suppress my embarrassment and share a small sampling with you here.

(These extracts are all quite genuine, and the originals are available for scholarly inspection; but, by leaving out the names, perhaps I can avoid the risk of finding that some of the writers may subsequently have changed their minds.)

"I picked up a copy of one of your books the other day in a doctor's office, and it probably did me more good than the doctor." — *Kelso, Washington*

"Your book is a great invention . . . . My mother is such a bore, and she just doesn't ever laugh! So she found this book — and she just laughed until midnight! . . . Thanks for helping my mother to laugh again!" — *Eugene, Oregon*

"You fill a terrific need in this world with your wit, humor, and stabs in the back." — *Arvada, Colorado*

"I think POT-SHOTS® are better than a university class in Philosophy." — *Drayton Plains, Michigan*

"This past weekend my uncle passed away. He was what you might call conservative and just slightly right wing. But like all of us he obtained great pleasure from your work. He thought you were amazing! Your humor passes all political and social boundaries." — *Brentwood, N.Y.*

"When I read your thoughts, I feel love. . . . I enjoy being in your head." — *Upper Sturt, S.A., Australia*

"Being a 75-year old widower, I have for some time been sending . . . . your choice POT-SHOTS® to my first love of 50 years ago in attempts to persuade her to start a new life with me before it is too late." — *Santa Barbara, California*

"Anyone who puts out postcards saying things like "THE TIME FOR ACTION IS PAST — NOW IS THE TIME FOR SENSELESS BICKERING [#1019] probably shares numerous experiences with me." — *Massachusetts Institute of Technology*

"I must thank [you] for helping me acquire my present job. By splattering assorted verbiage (acquired from several postcards) on my application, I was able to give the employers the incredible impression that I was intelligently insane. Thus I am now a business manager for a group dental practice." — *Belmont, California*

"After our earthquake, I was feeling quite shaken for days and depressed. I realized I needed some help, and recommended to myself that I get your books out and read a bit from time to time. I now have one downstairs and one upstairs. It's working." — *San Jose, California*

"I've discovered your book . . . in a friend's bathroom last week, and had the funniest time I've ever had in a bathroom before!"
— *Quathioski Cove, B.C., Canada*

"There were times when I seriously considered 'throwing in the towel.' When I felt that way, along came your 'saying' in my local paper in a most unique wording that made me stop and think. . . . I truly believe it helped save my life." — *Belle Chasse, Louisiana*

"I recently read your book when my friend transcribed it into braille for me. Even without the benefit of the pictures I enjoyed every word and thought."
— *Jamaica, N.Y.*

"I'm glad your limit to 17 words [sic] as that is really all I can handle."
— *Anchorage, Alaska*

"I am a receptionist in a Real Estate office. . . . I had to be asked to put your book down, for I was so engrossed in reading that I didn't realize my phone was ringing and ringing." — *Saratoga, California*

"I am a great admirer of your interpretive art, which, as a psychiatrist, I can fully appreciate. It might interest you to know that I have used your POT-SHOTS® to highlight therapeutic interpretations to patients." — *Detroit, Michigan*

"When my husband saw your book, he laughed for the first time in months. The unfamiliar sound was music to my ears. Thank you." *Hood River, Oregon*

"Your books . . . have been shared with anyone who would put out a hand or mind to pick them up, including an entire high school English department and a Catholic priest who was almost tempted enough to be light-fingered." — *Winnebago, Illinois*

"I wanted you to know that, though your book did not save my life (that may come later), it did give my morale a good kick in the pants." — *Corvallis, Oregon*

"These jottings. . . help me live a clean and sober life by not letting the 'STINKING THINKING' get me down." — (PFC, U.S. Army).

"Your book . . . gave me solace, sort of a Balm in Gilead to divert me from the problem of becoming 65 all at once, for which I'd received no earlier training. (I expect to be 65 for several months, then, I'm told, it will go away)." — *Bay City, Michigan*

"The cards out-class any one I know and more important still, they will last through generations of literate and educated people the world over." — *Lagos, Nigeria*

"No man could have the compassion and insight qualities that you apparently have. Please verify your sex for us." — *Latrobe, Pennsylvania*

"Almost everything I read in your POT-SHOTS is something I've been thinking somewhere in my stomach or insides somewhere, and just couldn't get out." — *Alma, Michigan*

"I am an 18 year old girl who just left behind her past in Washington to begin a future in California. Since my arrival, my spirits have been somewhat down. I went to take a nap on the couch when I saw Grandma's books piled on the coffee-table. I saw your book, and decided to open the cover and read the pages. To my surprise, when I was finished, I felt so good I could have walked right out of my front door and conquered the world!" — *Placentia, California*

"Hey! You're alright for a White guy! . . . Keep the faith, Partner!" — *Novi, Michigan*

"I never heard of you until a few weeks back, yet I feel as if you had been living in my head for 3 or 4 decades." — *Clearlake, Washington*

"I absolutely love your lines. Reading them during my nervous breakdown allowed me to laugh about myself and with you, and helped me to accept and heal. That is honestly true." — *New York, N.Y.*

"I do a variety of lecturing, and have found the cards useful and entertaining. They are wonderful examples of how to use humor to alleviate stress and build self-esteem." — *Davenport, Iowa*

"My romance with my boyfriend was going downhill, but POT-SHOTS® are helping us to communicate . . . in a fun and exciting way. We leave POT-SHOTS® in each other's cars." — *East Detroit, Michigan*

"I have a stern Scots appearance and people don't realize that underneath I have an irrepressible sense of humor, [but] now I have a wonderful collection of your cards to prove it." — *Kenilworth, Cape Provincè, South Africa*

"All the manic-depressive schizoid existential pseudosurrealists I know love your postcards — the best thing since Valium, and more portable than bathroom walls." — *Berkeley, California*

"I found your book . . . at a conference on 'The Power of Laughter and Play'. . . . I keep finding new ways to include POT-SHOTS,® even in the presentations I do in the field of death and dying." — *Miami, Florida*

"I am a postal clerk. . . and have been following your POT-SHOTS® for some time. . . . It has been quite a while since the front of a postcard was better than the back." — *New York, N.Y.*

"You are in my newspaper — and POT-SHOTS® are the high point of all the words the paper offers." — *Houma, Louisiana*

"I use your POT-SHOTS® to carry on a discussion with my . . . foreign born students. I find the words easy and well suited for my students' level of understanding of the English language." — *Dearborn, Michigan*

"I'm in a play right now in college, and I'd like to give the cast and crew gifts of your postcards on opening night. I think it would be a great way of breaking the tension." — *Bronx, N.Y.*

"I thought my wife was insane reading your books, so I read one, and now we both are." — *Sunnybank Hills, Queensland, Australia*

"When my mother died (81 years) we found hundreds of your little POT-SHOTS® filed away in her desk. One of her grandsons made a little stand to sit on the baby grand piano, and every day she put your current Pot-Shot up. If she was not too impressed with today's, she filed through and got one of her favorites out of the backlog. Thanks for entertaining her through her last years." — *Algonac, Michigan*

Mailed Fist

But paens of praise are of course not the whole story, and I do occasionally get the postal equivalent of a punch in the nose. Here are some choice specimens:

"Your...ugh...'cartoons,' I have noticed over the months, are *BRILLIANTLY DEPRESSING*! Oftentimes I just pass over it. . . because I've found that chances are it will *be* depressing. But this one [#4375 — see p.132] had the word GOD in it, so I gave it the benefit of the doubt. And was, of course, promptly let down. The groveling self-pity is . . . just *nauseating*. Why don't you get into another line of work? Like, say, garbage collection or sewer maintenance? Such surroundings would seem to fit your mind-set. . . . Pardon me, but you really are a jerk, you know that? . . . Get a life, dude, or get out of the mass media." — *Eagle River, Alaska*

"Everything you ever say is a cliche. . . . Your attempts at humor are about as humorous as a ball of lint hidden behind an empty box of trash can liners. . . .The space wasted on your 'cube of wit' implies that you have something to say, which you never do. The mental level required to appreciate [you] is roughly that of an idiot coming down off of a drug trip while suffering appendicitis and a migrain simultaneously." — *Seattle, Washington*

"I really don't know why I go on reading your POT-SHOTS® . . . I always have the annoyed reaction of — how can anyone's head be screwed on backwards to *that* degree?" — *Montecito, California*

Loose End

Welcome back to (or from) reality! (#1385)

I hope you enjoyed our eventful journey, and that, as a result of it, your general condition has improved, or at least not seriously deteriorated. We now face the task of re-entry, which is not always easy, especially when it isn't clear exactly what we are re-entering.

But even though we all have to disembark here, this, of course, is not really the end of the line. In fact, you can connect at this point with many more of my lines, in the form of postcards, books, and other Brilliant products. If (as I fondly hope) this prospect excites you, I invite you to send for my Catalogue (a masterpiece in itself), which comes with sample cards and an alluring order-form. The current (1990) price is two U.S. dollars. Please enclose that amount, or its equivalent in your own time and currency. My address is:

Ashleigh Brilliant
117 W. Valerio St.,
Santa Barbara, California 93101
U.S.A.